To Me, He Was Just Dad

To Me, He Was Just Dad

Stories of Growing Up with Famous Fathers

Joshua David Stein

AND THE EDITORS OF **FATHERLY**

ARTISAN | NEW YORK

Contents

Introduction

THIS BOOK WAS INSPIRED BY A CONVERSATION with Ethan Wayne, son of legendary actor John Wayne. Ethan had written a story for Fatherly.com in which he described toddling around small Mexican towns on the Sea of Cortez hand in hand with his famously imposing father. This image was so at odds with the Duke's popular persona— the squinting, the smoking, the stoicism—that it made us curious: *How wide*, we wondered, *is the gap between what the public thinks of notable men and what the sons or daughters of those men experience? Do great men make for great fathers? What about terrible men? And what can we, who likely fall somewhere in between, learn from those answers?*

We at Fatherly are journalists obsessed with fathers and the experience of fatherhood, so we did the only logical thing: We asked. We sought out the children of renowned scientists, athletes, musicians, innovators, and even criminals. We collected happy memories and a handful of regrets. We heard stories that surprised us, and a few that didn't. (Jeff Bridges turns out to be exactly who you'd hope. Pablo Escobar was a doting dad. Samuel L. Jackson is a nerd. Kurt Vonnegut was a sucker for board games.) We learned that public acclaim for a man both matters to his children and, at the same time, profoundly does not. We discovered how the by-products of fame— money, shame, the demands of the public—can transform a child's life and thinking.

What follows are essays about the private lives of public men written by their grown children. Taken all together, these pieces are about not just famous fathers but also relative velocity—that is, the ways in which families speed along together, even as they become blurs to the watching world. Many of the men profiled here were luminaries and leaders, men who moved fast. But the kids sitting on their laps saw them as steady hands. They saw in them goodness as well as greatness.

The writers of these essays remember their fathers playing catch, not pro ball; sitting on picnic blankets, not prestigious boards; giving praise, not receiving it. They remember patience, kindness, and humor—and the longing they felt when those qualities were absent.

They also remember their fathers trying to balance professional and paternal ambition. Sometimes successfully, sometimes not. After all, many of the men featured in this book were monomaniacal. This was readily apparent to their children, who struggled to calibrate their fathers' renown with their own needs. Many now hold on to the moments they spent in the company of their dads with much more tenderness and care than they do these men's outward achievements.

For fathers, this book begs a question about how *we* will be remembered. What stories will our children tell? What will they have to say about the sacrifices we made and those that we didn't? What will they think of our life's work? As these essays show, in the formulation "My Father the _____," "my father" is by far the more important descriptor than whatever fills the blank.

If the stories in this book are any indication, our children will remember quiet moments—reading together, curling up on the couch—and adventures alike. They will also remember when we didn't show up and what we were doing at the time. Everything will be recorded. How they will calibrate these feelings is impossible to predict. But hopefully, they will see time spent with us as proof that they were loved—and they will remember their fathers moving with speed and purpose but never leaving them behind.

My Father the All-Star Kareem Abdul-Jabbar

by Habiba Alcindor

Born Ferdinand Lewis Alcindor Jr. in New York City in 1947, Kareem Abdul-Jabbar is widely considered one of the greatest basketball players of all time. He was named the NBA's Most Valuable Player a record six times and is the league's all-time leading scorer with 38,387 points. In addition to being an athlete, Abdul-Jabbar is an actor and author. In 2016, he was awarded the Presidential Medal of Freedom by Barack Obama. He has five children, Habiba, Sultana, Kareem Jr., Amir, and Adam.

Everyone in Los Angeles got swept up in Lakers Mania in the early 1980s. Magic Johnson and my dad were huge celebrities. But they were also really different men, and my father didn't benefit from the comparison. Magic was friendly and well-liked—he was always having parties at his huge house or throwing them at Lakers owner Jerry Buss's estate in Beverly Hills. My dad lived in Bel-Air. We didn't even know the neighbors. Win or lose, my dad didn't want to be bothered. He wanted to go home and be by himself.

The flashiest thing in my father's house was an Andy Warhol portrait of him based on a Polaroid Warhol had taken. Otherwise the place was typical for the era. It was a one-story bungalow with Persian carpets everywhere, a Jacuzzi in the bathroom, and a room full of records. I have a lot of memories of my father spending hours in that room, listening to music, or in his bedroom, watching television. I grew up mostly with my mom, but my siblings and I spent summers with my dad. He often seemed distant and disconnected from us children, even though he complained bitterly about our mom having been awarded custody of us.

My brothers would try to bond with my dad by listening to jazz with him. I never did. I hate jazz. Part of the reason is that my dad would put on discordant acid jazz and speed down Sunset Boulevard in his Mercedes-Benz. I associate those old albums with feeling queasy. Weird episodes like that defined our relationship when I was young.

My dad wasn't just weird with me. He was weird with everyone. He wasn't a status-conscious person who performed for other famous people. His closest friends weren't who you'd expect. They were Lou Adler, who produced *The Rocky Horror Picture Show*, and Richard Rubinstein, who made *Pet Sematary*. That wasn't because my dad wanted to be an actor. He never took an acting class, never asked Lou or Richard for roles (though Richard did cast him as a genie in an episode of *Tales from the Darkside*). He just got along well with them. Richard shared my dad's love of the Dune series and eventually bought the film rights to make a miniseries. Lou, who produced Carole King's *Tapestry*, also owned the Roxy Theatre, a famous LA nightclub, so he and my dad bonded over music. Richard and Lou accepted that my dad didn't understand the concept of returning favors. The people who stayed friends with my dad all *really* wanted to be able to call him a friend.

If my father had lived a normal life, I think he would have caught on more quickly that he didn't have normal relationships with people. But because he was very tall and very famous and black, he didn't have normal relationships with anyone anyway. No one knew how to handle him, but they wanted to be his friend—even if he treated them poorly or was aloof, which he often was. Since he was that way with everyone, I didn't take his behavior personally. Nevertheless, it hurt.

Even before my parents divorced, the NBA schedule kept my dad away from home. During my childhood, there wasn't a continuity to his presence. Though I vaguely knew that his whereabouts were tied to the basketball season, mostly it felt like he just showed up and then was gone. This makes it hard to talk about my father, since building the story is like sorting through random film clips. I remember attending the premiere of *Airplane!* with him and thinking that we were just going to a movie. My siblings and I tried to play some basketball with him, but he wouldn't let us get the ball. My dad taught me to ride a bike, and he taught me to play baseball. He did those things. He just disappeared for months in between.

Still, I was proud of him. I called him Big Daddy when I was really young and basked in his stature. One time when I was playing at the park, a boy got on the slide in front of me. He stood at the top of the ladder and said I couldn't come up. I was upset, so I told him I was going to get my daddy. And I did. My father showed up, and suddenly the kid was looking Kareem Abdul-Jabbar, this seven-foot-tall man, straight in the eyes. My dad was very matter-of-fact. He told the kid he could slide down the slide or get knocked down it. My dad would

Habiba (age sixteen), Sultana (age nine), and Kareem, 1988

never have hit the kid, but for me, his daughter, he could be threatening when he wanted to be.

My brothers and sister were willing to remain silent in order to get along with my dad; I wasn't, which contributed to his impression that I was a troublesome child. For example, I'd demand to know why he didn't call on my birthday. Whenever he failed to live up to my expectations, I would get emotional and tell him, which made him uncomfortable.

Changing my name didn't help, either. My siblings and I were born into the Hanafi Muslim community outside Washington, DC, which was intensely isolated. We grew up observant, but I don't consider myself Muslim. The name Abdul-Jabbar was, from my perspective, a name handed to my father by a spiritual leader of a religion toward which I felt ambivalent. When I was seventeen, I made the decision to change my last name to Alcindor—my father's family name—and asked my mom to sign the legal documents. A story about it ran in the *National Enquirer*, and my dad threw a fit. To this day, I don't think he's forgiven me, but I hope he's made peace with it.

For years, my father was at the epicenter of the universe that is Los Angeles. But that never changed the way he saw the world or himself. He was always 100 percent himself, for better or for worse. I think I'm like my dad. I freeze people out. I can be a little standoffish. But there are good things I've gotten from him as well. I'm not status conscious—I like people for unpredictable reasons. I always thought that was a nice thing about my dad. Most important, though, I've learned to be myself, unapologetically and always.

───────────

Habiba Alcindor is a journalist, filmmaker, screenwriter, and radio talk show host who lives in the Bronx, New York. She is the creator and writer of the dramatic series *Gold Rush*.

My Father the Bad Motherf*cker

Samuel L. Jackson

by Zoē Jackson

Samuel L. Jackson is the all-time highest-grossing box-office star. Born in 1948 in Washington, DC, Jackson was raised in Chattanooga, Tennessee. His early filmography includes Jungle Fever *and* Juice, *but it was his role as Jules Winnfield in Quentin Tarantino's* Pulp Fiction *that turned Jackson into a cultural touchstone. Since then he's starred in many of Tarantino's films as well as in the Star Wars and Avengers series. He has one daughter, Zoē, and lives in Los Angeles, California, with his wife, LaTanya Richardson.*

Zoë (age four) on her way to school with Samuel, 1986

MY FATHER IS A BIG NERD, in the best way possible. He is completely different from his cool-guy persona. He's got a wormhole personality in that he burrows into whatever strange thing he's interested in and gets *really* into it. After we moved to Los Angeles when I was ten, we would go to Golden Apple Comics on Melrose every week religiously. They even kept a pull box for my dad. (A pull box is something that only comic book nerds have—the store pulls the new comics on a customer's list and keeps them behind the counter.) I used to be into all things Archie, but Dad's pull box was full of weird and really violent comics that I wasn't allowed to read. Dad and I didn't start exchanging comic books until I got to college. I forced him to read The Sandman (the Neil Gaiman reboot). He forced me to read the neo-noir series 100 Bullets, the western Scalped, and WildStorm's The Boys. When I was in college, whenever I went to the comic book store alone, I was sad. I wanted my dad to be there.

Before we moved to LA, I spent a lot of time with my father. Both my parents are actors—back then working primarily in theater—and at that time, my mom was the busier, better known of the two. My dad took me to school every single day: We would get on the subway in Harlem, ride it downtown to a crosstown bus, and then transfer to another bus until we got to the Upper West Side. We would also go to the Bronx Zoo together. My dad loves animals: reptiles, mammals, fish. He especially loves snakes. He was full of animal facts—he actually studied marine biology in college.

Though I was largely shielded from it at the time, my dad was struggling with addiction during much of my childhood. When I was eight, he entered rehab. He was gone for sixty days, which was a confusing time for me. I had no idea anything was wrong. Now, when I look back on that time, I don't know to what to attribute some of my memories. I remember going to a bar on the Upper West

Side with my dad. He'd give me a quarter and I'd go play "Tequila" by the Champs in the jukebox on repeat. (I was really into *Pee-wee's Playhouse*.) But I never saw him drunk that I know of. I just thought he was a dude who slept a lot.

We moved to Los Angeles for my mom. She got a role in the short-lived Chuck Lorre series *Frannie's Turn*. But soon my dad's career really took off, and my mom stopped working as much to take care of me. It's funny that my father is the better-known actor, because my mom was the one who pushed him to act in the first place. They met in a professor's office at Morehouse. (My dad went to Morehouse; my mom went to Spelman. The teacher taught at both colleges.) Dad was looking for extra credit, and Mom was doing some makeup work. She said, "You need to be in my play. Do you act?" Dad said, "Actually, I don't," but my mom replied, "Well, you do now." And that's how it went, and how it has gone ever since. My mom turns the key and sends Dad out into the world. He comes back and seeks her opinion, and she's happy to advise. They've been married for close to fifty years now. She still gives him notes on his performances. They can't live without each other. They each send me articles about the other. I do think it was very hard for my mom to give up her career to raise me for as long as she did, though. She's happy for my dad, of course, but it's complicated. There's a sadness there.

I was twelve years old when *Pulp Fiction* came out. After that, my dad became cool. Or, he thought he did. And though much of the world agrees, he's still just a big nerd to me. He goes through phases. Now it's watching Korean martial arts movies and Thai B movies. He reads four or five books about random topics at once. And now he DMs me all the time on Instagram and recommends obscure trap music and stuff. Once, he gave me a sweatshirt he got from working on *Django Unchained*. He said, "I signed it for you!" I was like, "Dad, thanks. Now I can't wear it!" It's up to my mom and me to pull him back down to earth. I mean, isn't that what family's for?

Zoë Jackson is an Emmy Award–nominated television producer and director. She lives in New York City.

My Father the Beatle John Lennon

by Julian Lennon

John Lennon was a songwriter and musician, born in Liverpool, England, in 1940. Together with his friends Paul McCartney, George Harrison, and later Ringo Starr, he was a member of the Beatles, one of the most popular and influential bands in the world. He was assassinated in 1980 in New York City and is survived by his sons, Julian and Sean, and his second wife, Yoko Ono.

John and Julian (five years old) posing in front of John's psychedelic Rolls-Royce, in Liverpool, UK, 1968

ALOT OF MY HAPPY MEMORIES of my father are from the late 1960s at Kenwood, the old Tudor house we had in Surrey, England, when I was a little boy. The house had a front-room lounge with windows that faced west where I used to watch the sunset. That was the main hang. Without knowing it, I probably saw some of the greatest musicians in the world come and go through that room.

I remember sitting on the roof of that house with my dad making a balsa-wood airplane. There was a great view from up there. As a kid, I thought my dad was pretty happy—with the family, the family home, and his place in the world. Who could have predicted that everything was about to change?

The Beatles had just released *Sgt. Pepper's Lonely Hearts Club Band*. At the time, my dad had his famous psychedelic Rolls-Royce Phantom V, which I adored because it had a record player in the back. We also had a Honda monkey bike, a mini motorcycle we used to ride around on. Ringo lived down the road, and my dad would take me to see him on the monkey bike. My dad had a great sense of humor. He loved Peter Sellers and had a comedic sensibility I naturally shared. You see it in some of his sketches and in his book *A Spaniard in the Works*.

At Kenwood, my father and I were close. So close, in fact, that though my first name is also John, I started to get called Julian or Jules since when my mum would shout, "John, your dinner's ready!" both my dad and I would react. Then suddenly he literally disappeared off the face of the planet. At least, that's how it seemed to me. He and Yoko Ono were deeply, and publicly, in love. And I felt like my mum and I had been cast aside. Not everyone forgot about us, though. Paul wrote "Hey Jules" after dropping in to check how my mum and I were doing. (Obviously, the title of the song changed.)

Maybe ten years passed during which my dad and I barely spoke. I was very angry about how he left the family. It was thanks to my mum that we started having conversations again. She was such a gentle soul, never vindictive in any way, shape, or form. My mum got brushed off, and she struggled with it for years, but she always wanted me to have a relationship with my dad.

I was scared the first time I went to visit him in the United States after my parents' divorce. I was becoming more aware of the magnitude of this man. I was fixated on an episode that had occurred years before during a trip to Montauk, when he became very angry at me for laughing. I had an uncontrollable nervous giggle as a child, which upset him a great deal. My dad had berated me, telling me to shut up. So I was worried about that. Much to my relief, the visit was a success. There was a lot of laughter—but not from nervousness. My dad was charming and funny and warm. From that trip on, I remember us getting along better. We had some good times after that, less as father and son but more as friends, or maybe a combination of both.

In fact, I often return to another memory, one that reminds me of the time we made the balsa-wood plane at Kenwood. In 1979, the remains of Hurricane David were coming toward Long Island, and I was standing with my dad on the lawn at a rented house near Montauk. There were 100-kilometer winds sweeping through, and my half brother, Sean, was with us. We were just enjoying one another's company, watching the storm approach, and I recall it was the first day we all spent together.

Even though I was playing guitar before I was in my teens, I hesitated to enter the music business because of who my dad was. I would send him the odd cassette of me playing live, or song ideas I had recorded on a little Sony Walkman he had given me as a gift. He warmly encouraged me to continue playing, but sadly, he never really got to see my career unfold, as he passed when I was seventeen. When I did finally become a professional musician a few years later, I felt like I understood him better. I experienced just a fraction of the mania that he did, but I got a sense of what it's like when thousands of people are waiting outside your hotels, trying to rip off your clothes when you come or go. I can't imagine going through that with a wife and kid at home.

I can certainly understand why my dad did a lot of what he did, particularly in terms of keeping his emotions bottled up inside, hidden especially from those he loved. The Lennon men seem to be always running off, singing and playing the guitar, looking for a way to express ourselves. I understand the frustration my dad had when it came to that, and I'm grateful that at least he found his way through his music. I just wish he could have done that a bit more with me, as a father, too.

I try to remember my dad as fondly as possible. I strive for forgiveness and understanding in that area of my life, for the difficult times he put my mum and me through. I loved her more than anything and can't forget how poorly he treated her. But our relationship was getting better before he died. He was in a happier place. He wanted to reconnect, not just with me but with the rest of his family in Scotland, Wales, and Ireland. He never got a chance to do so. Even now, almost forty years after my father died, and almost five years after my mum passed away, I try to hold my father's memory dear. I imagine that's what he would have wanted. That's what my mum would have wanted. And that's what I would like, too.

Julian Lennon is a musician and photographer and the founder of the White Feather Foundation.

My Father the Captain

Peter Willcox

by Natasha Willcox

Peter Willcox, born in Vermont in 1953 and raised in Connecticut, is a sea captain best known for his work with Greenpeace. In more than thirty-five years with the environmental organization, he participated in some of its most notable campaigns: He was the captain of the Rainbow Warrior *when it was bombed in New Zealand in 1985, and in 2013, he—along with twenty-nine others, together called the Arctic Thirty—was arrested by Russian authorities while sailing in the Pechora Sea; he was held for two months. He has two daughters, Natasha and Anita, from his first marriage and a stepson, Skylar Purdy, with his second wife, Maggy Aston.*

I WAS BORN IN SPAIN, but when I was six, my parents separated, and my dad moved back to the United States. My sister and I would spend the summers with him. Then, when I was ten, we moved to the States to live with my dad full-time. I was very excited and curious about what that would be like.

Papa, as we call him, worked at Greenpeace, but beyond knowing that it was a really cool organization that did wonderful things for the environment and for our planet, I don't think I fully understood what that meant. I realized that my father's work came with risks, but also that he was extremely dedicated to it. I remember hearing my dad tell the story of the *Rainbow Warrior*, a Greenpeace ship that was bombed by French intelligence and sank off the coast of New Zealand. Dad was on board and narrowly escaped drowning. (One photojournalist was killed.) But that hadn't dissuaded my father from his mission.

Everyone at Greenpeace calls my dad Pete. At home, his friends call him Peter. Pete Willcox and Peter Willcox are two different people. At work, my father is in his element. He's an amazing sailor and a great captain. He's passionate about the environment and the work he does. He's most comfortable when he's aboard a ship.

He's different as a dad. A lot of the qualities that make someone a stellar ship captain do not necessarily make them the best parent. On a ship, in order to remain calm and collected under immense pressure, the captain has to be emotionally removed. For my father, raising two daughters on his own was probably hard enough, but it was made doubly difficult by the fact that his way of dealing with his feelings was to keep them locked up. By the time my sister and I moved to the United States, we were entering that age at which, naturally, we had a lot of questions and a lot of struggles. Being a teenage girl is confusing. Papa was not particularly equipped to have those difficult conversations, not just factually but, more important, emotionally.

There were no answers he could give, no easy solutions to our problems. He had to just listen and be present. It was new and challenging for him.

When we first arrived, Papa was really trying to be with us fulltime. He was teaching sailing classes and coaching my softball and soccer teams. But by the time I got to high school and my sister, Anita, was starting college, he was shouldering a much greater financial burden and needed a job that offered more hours and would bring in a steady income. That's when he rejoined Greenpeace. There were months-long stretches when he would be gone and I would stay with my aunt and uncle. I remember a lot of people looking down on him for that. A big part of me was upset about it, too. He was not the best at communicating when he was on the ship, so I would sometimes go a little too long without hearing from him. But looking back on it now, I understand his decision to leave.

I was in my first semester of college, in 2013, when my dad was detained by the Russian government. I coped by burying myself in my studies as much as I could. I also kept telling myself: *It's Greenpeace! They get arrested all the time! It's no big deal!* That's what kept me afloat. But in October, when the Russian government charged my dad and the rest of the Arctic Thirty with piracy, I realized that things were much more serious. It occurred to me that I might never see my dad again. When I learned that the Russian authorities were talking about a sentence of many, many years, I thought, *He's not going to see me graduate from college. He's not going to see me get married. He's not going to see any of this.* All of that hit me at once. It was incredibly hard.

But our family has a really strong support system, and all the work my dad did for the public good came back to us. Anyone I had ever met from Greenpeace reached out on Facebook and said things like "I hope you are doing okay. We're all standing behind your dad and the Arctic Thirty. Please tell me if you need anything." People I had never met before offered to help, too. That warmed my heart so much. It felt like all these people were putting their hands on my shoulder, comforting me. I tear up every time I think about those messages.

Natasha (one year old) and Peter, 1995

The day the Russian government dropped the piracy charge in favor of the much less serious "hooliganism," I was sitting in the dining hall after crew practice. One of my friends walked in, and from across the room, I heard, "Natasha! What the heck is hooliganism?!" I just burst out laughing.

What else is there to know about my dad? His favorite ice cream flavor is chocolate. He snores in a really funny way; it's less like snoring and more like little puffs of air. He loves the show *The West Wing*. (He got me and my sister into it. I owe him for that.) He loves Bruce Springsteen. He read the whole Harry Potter series to me and Anita out loud, multiple times. When I watch the movies, I hear a lot of the lines in the voices my dad did instead of how the actors are saying them.

I have a great memory from when I was quite young. My dad and I were hiking somewhere in Spain. I remember him sitting against a pine tree, and it being kind of windy. He said, "I love that sound."

"What sound?" I asked.

"The sound of the wind blowing through pine needles. It sounds just like the ocean," he replied.

It really does. Every time I hear the wind blowing through pine needles, I hear his voice in my head saying that.

Natasha Willcox is a horticulturist for R. P. Marzilli & Company. She lives in Hopkinton, Massachusetts.

My
Father
the
Cartoonist
Garry
Trudeau

by Ross Trudeau

Garry Trudeau, born Garretson Beekman Trudeau in New York City in 1948, is the creator of the comic strip Doonesbury, *for which he became the first cartoon strip artist to win a Pulitzer Prize, in 1975. Trudeau has also written and produced films and television shows, including* Tanner '88 *and the political satire* Alpha House. *He married journalist Jane Pauley in 1980, and they have three children, Ross, Rachel, and Thomas.*

N EXT TO THE DOOR of my father's studio stood a lacquered mahogany grandfather clock that didn't work. It was at the end of a hall that ran the length of our tenth-floor apartment in New York. If the studio door was closed, I would sometimes open the clock's cabinet door and set its brass pendulum swinging, producing a resonant *tick-tock* that softened as gravity took its course.

Tick-tock. Knock-knock.

"Just a minute, Rossy."

Dad only ever seemed to shut the studio door on Fridays. His slate of six dailies and one nine-panel Sunday strip were all due to the inker by 6:00 p.m. that day, and he rarely finished a minute earlier. And just as his professional anxiety reached its weekly zenith, we three children would get home from school and burst into the pre-war Central Park West co-op with typical weekend-anticipatory zeal. The few times my father could have been said to have snapped at me unfairly occurred at the threshold of his studio, at mid-afternoon on a Friday: deadline day (or, as my sister, Rachel, called it, "Daddy's Mad Day").

While it was by no means off-limits, the studio was a serious place and held an appeal that, for most of my childhood, defied naming. For although it was a space for hard work and sustained concentration, it was at the same time filled to bursting with objects that looked for all the world like toys: a wooden Dan Quayle figurine that ejected an erect penis when you picked it up; a hand-carved didgeridoo; a life-size papier-mâché sculpture of Mike Doonesbury's head and torso; USO press lanyards from Iraq and Kuwait; amorphous gummy wads of gray eraser material that turned white and shredded like dough when you stretched them out.

The studio had the power to subtly transform my father. He was an affectionate man, an enthusiastic roughhouser, and capable of unabashed silliness. But inside the studio, he seemed more solemn, more focused, more staid. More like Grandpa.

Dr. Francis B. Trudeau was a Columbia-trained country physician, a committed outdoorsman, and a decorated veteran of a US Navy subchaser. He was reserved but not aloof. Patrician but not domineering. Above all things, he valued honesty, respect, and integrity. And like my father's studio would years later, Grandpa's study in the upstate New York house where he raised his family served as a neat metonymy for the man.

The walls displayed a prized brook trout caught in Quebec, barometers and thermometers that he consulted daily, a painting of an Adirondack mountainscape. There were built-in shelves filled with boxes of delicate trout flies, and twin gun closets with a dozen hunting rifles between them. (Grandpa taught my father at age eight to shoot, clean, and oil a .22 but refused to ever buy him a BB gun on the grounds that he might treat it like a toy.) There was a flip-top desk and a low wooden coffee table with a bowl filled with Olympic pins from his time as the US Olympic ski team doctor at the Lake Placid Games. And at the center of the room, in front of the small fireplace, was a green leather armchair where every night Grandpa would dictate his medical notes into a Bell Dictaphone.

As a child, during family visits to Saranac Lake, I tried to steer well clear of Grandpa's study. My siblings and I were frightened by the alien solemnity of that room, where everything smelled of pleasantly stale Royal Yacht pipe tobacco. But to get to the guest bedroom where our parents slept, we had to summon the courage to pass through Grandpa's study, hoping he wasn't reading in his green chair. Though Grandpa never had anything but a broad smile for his grandchildren, disturbing him in his home office still felt profane. Here was a man whom my father still sometimes addressed as "sir," who was inevitably stopped for several embraces and handshakes when we went to Donnelly's for ice cream or to the tackle store before a fishing trip.

Grandpa's own grandfather, Dr. Edward Livingston Trudeau, had moved to the Adirondacks in 1873 to take the "rest cure"

Ross (age seven) and Garry at Lower Saranac Lake in the Adirondacks,
New York, 1990

after contracting tuberculosis. When he recovered, he remained in Saranac Lake, and in 1894 founded a TB sanatorium and the country's first laboratory for the study of the disease. (One of his early patients was Robert Louis Stevenson, who after his recovery gifted E. L. Trudeau his collected works; *The Strange Case of Dr. Jekyll and Mr. Hyde* bore the inscription, "With Trudeau these months at my side, I never caught a glimpse of Hyde.") Both E. L. Trudeau's son and grandson, Francis Sr. and Jr., would become doctors themselves. Francis Sr. eventually succeeded him as president of the sanatorium, and Frank Jr., my grandfather, stewarded it into its present-day incarnation as the Trudeau Institute, an independent immunology and infectious disease research center. While my father would himself become an active trustee of the institute, he would be the first Trudeau man in five generations not to get a medical degree.

Although my father's studio shared little aesthetically with his father's study, both rooms inspired in me a reverential awe. Whether looking up at Grandpa's medical volumes or at the *Time* covers above my father's sofa, I was filled with a similar dull dread that I would never know enough to be a man.

If I ever made a serious mistake—lied or failed to keep my word—I might hear my mother say, "Your father would like to see you in his studio." Punishment for fighting with my little brother or kicking my twin sister could be meted out on the spot. But lessons of character were taught in the studio.

When I was ten, Dad called me into his office after I had been caught in a lie about an antique teacup I had broken and then hidden. I sat in his artist's chair, teary and chastened and swiveling, staring at the indentations in the carpet where the wheels usually came to rest under his drawing board. "Things can be replaced, Ross. Hey, look at me." My father fixed on me with the same eyes that I have and that his father had before him: downward sloping at the temples, slightly hooded, suggesting melancholy or weariness. "We can glue this cup back together. But your reputation is more fragile and harder to fix. You only get one reputation."

When we had such serious studio talks, part of the enduring shame I felt at disappointing my father stemmed from the old-fashioned-sounding language he used. There among his Maoist propaganda pins, artifacts of the counterculture, and a poster of semi-stoned Zonker Harris, he would talk to me about reputation, honor, and "a man's word." I wouldn't have been able to articulate it this way then, but I understood him to be using a language passed down to him by his father.

The first time I can ever remember seeing my father cry is when he eulogized his father at St. John in the Wilderness at Lake Clear. It was 1995. Frank had died after a yearlong struggle with amyloidosis, though *struggle* is not perhaps the right word. In the year after his diagnosis, he was rarely in his study. Rather, he took to the slow rivers of Montana to go fly-fishing and sailed the twenty-foot boat he kept anchored off Saint John in the US Virgin Islands. My last glimpse of him was from the wharf off Cruz Bay.

At his father's funeral, Dad spoke about how Grandpa was immune to fashion, wearing the same clothes he had in college throughout his adult life. He remembered how his father had been touched by hours of spontaneous speeches of gratitude at a retirement dinner but how his only regret was that the speeches had focused almost entirely on his contributions to the institute, rather than his forty years as a physician meeting the day-to-day needs of his community of seven thousand in Saranac Lake. For decades, seven days a week with a break on Wednesday evenings, he was on call. Francis was there.

After his father was interred in the family plot—next to generations of his forebears going back to E. L. Trudeau—Dad brought just one token from Grandpa's study home with him: a desk name block from his days as an aide to a navy admiral.

While the simple wooden object never needed any explanation, it took years over the course of my childhood for the other eclectic artifacts in my father's studio to slowly come into focus. Dad never volunteered much information about those tchotchkes. I was well into my twenties when, while looking up at a portrait of Hunter S. Thompson, it occurred to me to ask Dad if he'd ever met the man he'd lampooned for decades. Dad said that no, he hadn't, but that he'd once received a package from Thompson filled with used toilet paper. I stood blinking at him, mouth open. He smiled and shrugged. I was thirty when I first commented on a pair of silk-screened portraits of him from the '70s—you can tell the era from his beard and leather cap—saying how much I liked them and didn't they look a lot like Warhols? Dad exhaled, tossing some junk mail in the wastebasket. Without turning around, he said that they were, in fact, original Warhols.

"No way. Stop it," I said.

"Well," Dad said, "he wasn't such a big deal back in those days."

My father says he has no interest in ever writing a memoir, claiming with apparent sincerity that he doesn't think anyone would be interested in reading the stories that lie behind the artifacts of his life. Are these things meaningful to him? Do they keep him company? Why do I, now a man myself, feel compelled to catalog them on his behalf? It's impossible not to wonder which of these objects might eventually end up on my desk or on the walls of my own home. Or perhaps I won't bring an object with me at all, just the memory of the soft echo of a grandfather clock in the hall. *Tick-tock. Knock-knock.*

Ross Trudeau is a crossword puzzle creator whose work is frequently published in the *New York Times*. He lives in Cambridge, Massachusetts.

My Father the Chef

Jacques Pépin

by Claudine Pépin

Jacques Pépin was born in Lyon, France, in 1935 and began working in his family's restaurant at age thirteen. He was the personal chef for three French heads of state, including Charles de Gaulle; worked at the legendary New York French restaurant Le Pavillon; and served for ten years as the director of research for Howard Johnson's. As the host of thirteen television shows— including Julia and Jacques Cooking at Home, *with Julia Child—Pépin taught much of America how to cook. He is the author of numerous books and has won two Emmys and twenty-four James Beard Foundation awards. He and his wife, Gloria, have one daughter, Claudine.*

I FEEL LIKE PAPA TAUGHT half of America how to make an omelet. He taught me how to make an omelet, too, and also how to walk, ski, and drive (that one was a touch stressful). But one of the most important things he taught me was how to be part of a deep and enduring friendship.

My father was twenty-two when he met twenty-year-old Jean-Claude Szurdak. It was 1957, and Papa was working as the chef for the French president, René Coty. He needed a pastry chef. Jean-Claude appeared at the kitchen door, a tall skinny kid who, as my father put it, "looked like a malnourished poet." Papa hazed him something terrible for the first twenty minutes, but he soon discovered that Jean-Claude was a well-trained and hardworking cook.

In 1959, my father moved to New York, and Jean-Claude soon followed. My father first worked at Le Pavillon and then as the director of research and development for Howard Johnson's while earning his master's degree in French literature at Columbia University. (My father always had an insatiable intellectual curiosity and read voluminously, from Molière to Camus.) Jean-Claude, meanwhile, started his own catering company. As a kid, I called him "Tonton Claude" and his wife "Tati Geneviève"—which is how French children would address their uncle and aunt. They were, and still are, part of our family. I consider their daughters cousins.

My father and Jean-Claude love each other like brothers, even though they sometimes pretend they don't, and they always take care of each other. Occasionally people assume they're a couple. They will often walk close together, and there is certainly no one else my father would trust more in the kitchen, or out of it. They're soul mates.

When I was five or six, Papa got into a terrible car accident while trying to avoid hitting a deer in Upstate New York. He ended up with fourteen fractures. At first, the doctors told my mother he wouldn't survive. Then they told her he'd survive but would never walk again. I remember at the time looking up at him in the hospital bed that would be his home for many months, and I was scared. Mom was there, of course, but so were Tonton Claude and Tati Geneviève. With their help and his own tenacity, three years later, my father started skiing again, of course in the company of Jean-Claude.

I don't believe that my father explicitly taught me about friendship. Instead, he spoke of loyalty. Of family. Of commitment. And by watching him and Jean-Claude together, I've learned that true friendship means calling your friend out on their bullshit but also, most important, being kind and generous and loyal.

––––––––––––

Claudine Pépin is a cookbook author and the cofounder and executive director of the Jacques Pépin Foundation. She lives with her husband and daughter in Barrington, Rhode Island.

Jacques and Claudine (two years old) at their home in Hunter, New York, 1967

My Father the Clown

Glen "Frosty" Little

by Tawnya Volz

Glen "Frosty" Little is among America's greatest whiteface clowns. Born in Genoa, Nebraska, in 1925, Little began his career with the Joe King Circus in Colorado in 1956. In 1968, he joined the first class of Ringling Bros. and Barnum & Bailey Clown College. He served as Boss Clown for Ringling for decades, eventually becoming director of clowns. In 1983, he was named Master Clown, one of only four clowns to hold that honor. He had two daughters, Tawnya and Roxanne. He died in 2010 at age eighty-four.

W HEN I WAS BORN, in 1951, my dad was working at the post office in Denver, Colorado. Before that he had served in the navy during World War II. But ever since he was a little boy growing up in Genoa, Nebraska, he wanted to be a clown. He had seen the circus when he was seven years old and had instantly fallen in love with the white-faced, red-nosed, kindhearted clowns.

When I was eight, my father and I began to dedicate our nights and weekends to clowning and performing. I was his sidekick, and I adored him. Every night after I did my homework, we would practice our juggling routines and new gags he had created for us to perform at our upcoming shows. Like most clowns, he was very serious when it came to the quality of his work and was a stickler down to the last detail. (In Dad's case, his fastidiousness didn't just apply to work, either. He'd fine me a nickel every time I left the toilet lid up! I learned very quickly not to do that.)

We would juggle Indian clubs, balls, and the like back and forth, but I was primarily the puppeteer. We had an interactive puppet show. Dad would be out with the crowd, and I was the one behind the curtain. Our show was so fun that it entertained not only children but adults as well. Over the course of a few years, we performed at hundreds of birthday parties and major entertainment venues throughout the Denver metropolitan area.

Working beside my father was a wonderful experience, and I marveled at how seamless my dad's show always was and how much he loved performing. He was a naturally gifted storyteller and a very charismatic man. He could convince a room full of kids that a length of rope on the floor was, in fact, a tightrope wire hundreds of feet in the air inside a circus arena. Kids would screw their faces up in intense concentration as they tried to walk on it, while others would cheer them on, and they would want to try it again immediately if they fell off.

Well before he became a famous clown, my dad was deeply devoted to being a *great* clown. I remember watching him apply his face makeup again and again, trying to come up with the perfect look. He told me that a clown's face is the most integral part of his costume. Dad always wanted to be a whiteface clown, in the tradition of Pierrot, rather than a hobo clown like his friend Emmett Kelly or a buffoon clown like Lou Jacobs. He's a sympathetic character but not a pathetic one.

When I was about eleven years old, Dad got a full-time job as a clown at Elitch Gardens, an amusement park in Denver. People would come from all over the country to dance at the famous Trocadero Ballroom, and there was my dad in his element, entertaining them. I even got to be part of his show with my own clown makeup, clown costume, and some gags. By that time, I had been performing with my dad for several years, and I loved it. Dad was demanding, sure, but that was because he cared that he presented perfection to the audience.

Everything changed for our family in 1968, when I was seventeen. That's when the Ringling Bros. and Barnum & Bailey Circus announced that they were starting a clown college in Sarasota, Florida. I don't think there was ever a question as to whether Dad would go. It had been his lifelong dream to be a clown for Ringling, and here was his chance. Before he left, I remember him sitting me down and telling me that he was moving and Mom and I weren't. (My mom, who for years had coordinated our shows in Denver, decided that she did not want a circus life, and my parents divorced.) But at that age, rather than being overcome with sadness, I just thought it sounded cool that my dad was joining the circus. "When am I coming to visit?" I asked. As it turned out, Dad was on the road so much that there wasn't a lot of time.

It was at the college that my dad found his perfect clown face and character. His dream had come true. After two years, Dad graduated and quickly became Boss Clown. Between touring the entire country with both Ringling units—there were two, the Red and the Blue, with their own trains and crews—and his growing responsibility, it

"Frosty" and Tawnya, 1973

was hard to keep in touch. I did get to visit him at the circus on different occasions on the road and could see that he expected the same quality of performance from his circus clowns as he had from me. Before each performance, he'd do a line-walk with them. "This wig looks sloppy!" "Take care of those shoes!" "Fix that makeup!" He ran Clown Alley as a tight unit, and the result was that his clowns were the best in the business.

In 1972, Dad remarried and continued performing with the circus, traveling with his second wife, Pat, in a camper with the train for years. In 1983, he was named a Master Clown. There was a ceremony in Washington, DC. It was a big deal. There have been only four Master Clowns in the history of Ringling. The Feld brothers, who owned the circus, inducted him. All of his friends were there in full clown makeup. Dad wore his makeup, too, and his costume—his small pointed red hat, a baggy red flannel suit, and oversize shoes. I think he was very moved and proud.

Over the years, I've thought a lot about my dad. The day clown college opened, the circus gained a Master Clown, but I was no longer his sidekick. Although I was not with him much after he joined the circus, I am proud to be Frosty Little's daughter. Clowning was what he was born to do. It was and always had been his dream, and I'm happy that he not only pursued that dream but also excelled at what he did.

I enjoyed every second of performing with him when I was young. Those years built a bond between us that could never be dissolved. Later, I watched as he touched the lives of thousands of people, and even from afar, I could feel his love.

Toward the end of his life, Dad developed Alzheimer's; the last time I saw him, in 2010, I was very sad that he no longer recognized me. For the most part, he was living again as if he was a boy. He was dreaming of the circus.

Tawnya Volz lives in the Denver, Colorado, metropolitan area. She is the mother of one daughter, a grandmother of four, and a great-grandmother of four. Now retired, she worked in business management, administration, and real estate sales.

My Father the Cover Artist Craig Braun

by Tim Braun

In the 1960s and '70s, graphic designer Craig Braun worked with the creative giants of his generation—Andy Warhol, Jimi Hendrix, and Led Zeppelin among them—to design album covers that were more than just pretty pictures. From the Velvet Underground banana sleeve to the Rolling Stones' lips and tongue logo, some of the century's most iconic images were produced by him. Born in Chicago, Illinois, in 1939 and now an actor living in Los Angeles, California, Braun has three sons, Tim, Nicholas, and Guillaume.

Craig and Tim (sixteen years old) in East Hampton,
New York, 1979

HERE'S A SNAPSHOT OF MY CHILDHOOD: my dad spilling out of a vintage Porsche in an embroidered goatskin coat and patchwork pants, a model on his arm, white powder visible under his nose. My dad loved—and lived—the rock-and-roll life. Whatever excesses that entailed, he only wanted more.

My parents were married just long enough to have me and realize that they weren't suited for each other *at all*. My mother and I lived in an apartment in Greenwich Village, while my dad, whom I saw on weekends, had a huge nineteenth-century carriage house on Sixty-Ninth Street between Third and Lexington Avenues. One of his girlfriends at the time, fashion designer Diane von Fürstenberg, called his place "the epitome of cool." It was pure '70s, chic and decadent, with lots of chrome and velvet, Jacuzzis, and a multilevel carpeted master suite strewn with mirrored Indian pillows.

Every night was a party. In the morning, I'd come downstairs to a sea of smudged glasses and ashtrays overflowing with still smoldering cigarette butts. Dad would stumble out of bed sometime later and we'd go for breakfast at his favorite place, the Barbizon Hotel. A women-only hotel famous for the beautiful actresses, airline stewardesses, and models who stayed there, the Barbizon had a coffee shop on the ground level that was open to the public. I'd hunker down with a pile of pancakes, submerging them in syrup, while Dad, through mirrored glasses, scoped out the "pie," looking for "new talent." His appetite was insatiable.

When I was nine, I was sent to the Malcolm Gordon School in Garrison, New York, an hour north of the city. It was a prim and proper all-boys boarding school, with ivy-covered walls and sweeping views of the Hudson River and West Point. On visiting day, at afternoon tea, the dads would sit with embroidered lime-green whales on their pants, their wives in simple madras shifts, while my dad sprawled in an armchair, shirt unbuttoned, legs splayed, never wearing underwear. When "the scene got too uptight," he would dis-appear into the bathroom and do a few lines of cocaine.

He was at the height of his fame then. His Rolling Stones *Sticky Fingers* album cover had just come out; he'd designed Alice Cooper's *School's Out*, which included a pair of disposable panties wrapped around every album, and Cheech and Chong's *Big Bambú* with its giant rolling paper. He was creating packaging and logos for almost every major act of the era—from Led Zeppelin and the Carpenters to Jimi Hendrix and the Beatles.

Being "hip" was essential to him, and he didn't miss a single fad, from Nehru jackets and Chelsea boots in the '60s to safari suits and platform shoes in the '70s. Sometimes he would show up with piles of clothes for me from Europe: tweed maxicoats with matching bell-bottom pants, flowered Liberty of London shirts, ribbed sweat-ers from France with buttons along the shoulder. Of course, my school required its students to wear a uniform, so I didn't have much use for any of it.

When I was eleven, he pulled me out of school for a last-minute trip to Europe with his French girlfriend, who was so beautiful, she literally stopped traffic. We went to London and Paris and Deauville, listening to Pink Floyd's *The Dark Side of the Moon*, Carly Simon's *No Secrets*, and Steely Dan's *Can't Buy a Thrill* on repeat on a portable turntable for the entire trip. Later that same year, my father won a Grammy for Best Art Direction/Design for the cover of the London Symphony Orchestra version of the Who's *Tommy* and brought the award up to show me at school. It turned out that there had been a mix-up backstage and he had somehow ended up with Carly Simon's Grammy for "You're So Vain." In retrospect, it's almost *too* easy to make a crack about that.

Watching this rock-and-roll lifestyle get the better of my dad was extremely painful. He really didn't have space in his life for a son and, because he always had to be the most handsome man in the room, didn't relish the idea of relinquishing attention to anyone else. Even me.

And then his world started to come apart in great chunks. In 1974, he was indicted by a grand jury for multiple counts of tax evasion and narrowly escaped going to prison. I found out about it while watching the nightly news in a room filled with my classmates. He started speedballing, snorting heroin laced with cocaine. His high-flying career took a nosedive.

By thirty-six, he was washed up, his design career finished.

Just when it seemed he couldn't sink any lower, he got lucky. A friend dragged him to an AA meeting in Los Angeles, and, somehow, the program stuck. He just celebrated forty years of sobriety.

As for me, after some therapy and a lot of introspection—along with a few years of not speaking to him—I've come to think of my dad as simply a toolbox that's missing a couple of tools. If I keep looking for them, I will continue to be disappointed. As long as I don't, we can have a relationship. There's no reason we should have a loving one, but we do—and he still can't believe it. He tells me how thankful he is almost every time we talk.

What I've learned is that you can't be mad at ghosts. He is not remotely the man I knew when I was a child anymore. I will not be one of those grown men or women who continues to blame their parents for the childhood they missed or the person they've become. It's my show now.

I am a very different sort of dad. I have twin teenage daughters and have relished celebrating and being totally involved in their lives.

Now whenever I see my dad's work, I feel proud of his accomplishments. I don't forget the tough times, but I feel fortunate that he survived those years and that my daughters can point to the Rolling Stones logo or the Velvet Underground banana peel and say, "Grandpa made that!"

Tim Braun is an award-winning executive producer, formerly of *Good Morning America*, and the founder of Braun Production, a video production company. He lives in Montclair, New Jersey, with his husband and their twin teenage daughters.

My Father the Cult Leader

Saul B. Newton

by Esther Newton

Born Saul Cohen in New Brunswick, Canada, in 1906, Saul B. Newton was an experimental American psychotherapist who led one of Manhattan's most infamous cults, the Sullivan Institute for Research in Psychoanalysis. From a sprawling Upper West Side complex, Newton forced members (called Sullivanians) to sever family ties, surrender control of their children, and engage in a nonmonogamous lifestyle. At the height of its popularity, in the 1970s, the institute counted hundreds of members, but by the '90s, beset by Newton's failing health and multiple lawsuits, it dissolved. Newton, who died at age eighty-five in 1991, was married—and divorced—six times and had ten children, of whom Esther is the eldest.

I F YOU KNOW ANYTHING ABOUT MY FATHER, Saul Newton, it's probably that he founded a group called the Sullivan Institute for Research in Psychoanalysis—a group that many people, myself included, came to view as a cult. For over thirty years, starting in 1957, Saul ran the institute with Jane Pearce, the woman for whom he left my mother when I was eight years old.

Saul wasn't my biological father, but he was the only father I knew. He came into the picture when I was six or seven. He was tall and very handsome, with big dark eyes and strong features. My biological father, a Communist named William Miller, refused to marry my mother, Virginia, because she wasn't Jewish. And so, Saul became my dad.

Saul moved in with my mother just after he returned from World War II. With his army uniform and the gun he had brought back from Europe kept in the closet, he was a big deal to me. I was very impressed by him and loved him immediately. By the time he left my mother, just a few years after he first came into our lives, he had already adopted me. So though he and my mother divorced, and he would go on to have many more wives and children, he was still my dad and clung to me for the rest of his life.

Saul, who had trained as a social worker, was heavily influenced by Harry Stack Sullivan, a neo-Freudian psychotherapist who believed that peer groups were just as important as families. What my father added to Sullivan's philosophy was a denunciation of the nuclear family—particularly, the mother-child bond—and, accordingly, a rejection of monogamy. He thought the secret to happiness was breaking up the family unit, and he created the institute on the Upper West Side as a place to put his philosophy into practice. All the therapists and patients who lived at the institute were forced to surrender to my dad's decisions when it came to raising—and conceiving—their own children. He would decide who should have children with whom, where they would live, and the rules by which they were raised.

Even though my dad preached against the family unit and ruthlessly enforced his philosophy with others, he exempted himself from his own teachings. In fact, he was a very engaged father. He taught me how to box, which wasn't traditional for a girl. He took me to the Macy's Thanksgiving Day Parade, where I sat on his shoulders to watch the floats go by. He taught me how to ride a bike and, when I was just seven years old, how to steer the family car.

As a young girl, I lived with my mother and was thus kept at arm's length from the activity at the institute. However, one summer, my father and Jane invited me to join them at the house they had built in Barnes Landing in Amagansett, New York. I remember that there was a group of shrinks and analysts who would come out. They'd hang out in the living room, which had lovely views of the bay, and drink—a lot. I presume, though I don't know for sure because I went to my bedroom to sleep, that they had sex with one another. That was my first exposure to my father's followers, and I was disgusted.

As a leader and as a father, Saul was tough. He had no patience for fear. I remember that the day he taught me to ride a bicycle, he sat me on the seat, and I was saying, "Daddy! Daddy! Don't let go." And he did, and I fell. And then he said, "Get back up. You can do it." And I did it. He also had a hideous temper and could become violent. One day, we went on a walk on a country path in Maine, where we spent our summers. Toward the end of it, I got tired, and I started to whine. That was something he hated. *Hated*. He took a stick off the ground and said, "You walk ahead of me, and if you get any closer to me than this stick, I'm going to hit you." The message, which I definitely absorbed, was that I had to toughen up.

My father used to rationalize everything. He'd say, "I need to lose my temper. It's good for my mental health." But it wasn't good for mine. When I was a teenager, I had a meltdown at a summer music camp. I was passionately in love with this girl who did not return my affection. I made a scene in the camp's dining room and they sent me to Austen Riggs, a psychiatric institution. I called my dad from there

Saul and Esther in New York City's Central Park, circa 1946

and he got on the phone and said, "What the fuck do you think you're doing?" It was tough love, but that was him. Eventually he came to pick me up.

My last conversation with my father was shortly before he died in 1991. He had dementia and couldn't recognize me. He had been kicked out by his sixth wife; he had been kicked out by his girlfriend. He had been kicked out of a nursing home and then a hospital for being violent. He had landed in a hospital in Brooklyn. My brother Rob and I were the ones who visited and brought him clean clothes. I was the one who, seeing that he was suffering, signed the DNR. When he died, I was the one who made sure he received an obituary in the *New York Times*. My dad was an amazing, complicated, brilliant individual. It was important to me that he wasn't remembered only as a nutjob with a cult. It was important that, though he spent decades trying to pry families apart, his family—at least I, his adopted daughter—was there for him.

Esther Newton is a cultural anthropologist best known for her pioneering work with the ethnography of lesbian and gay communities in the United States. She was a founding faculty member of SUNY's Purchase College and is currently a professor emerita of anthropology there. Her latest book is *My Butch Career: A Memoir*. She lives in Ann Arbor, Michigan, with her wife.

My Father the Daredevil Evel Knievel

by Robert Edward Knievel III

Evel Knievel, born Robert Craig Knievel in Butte, Montana, in 1938, was a professional daredevil. Known for his iconic white leather jumpsuits, Knievel held world records for the most cars and buses ever jumped over on a motorcycle for many decades. He also held the world record for the most bones broken in a lifetime (433). Knievel had four children, Kelly, Robert, Tracy, and Alicia. He died in 2007 at age sixty-nine.

Evel and Robert in Saint Petersburg, Florida, 1979

THE FIRST MEMORY I HAVE OF MY FATHER is from afar. I am a little boy, sitting in the stands with my mother at Ascot Park, a speedway outside of Los Angeles, gazing at the blurs of motorcycles speeding past. "Which one is Dad?" I ask.

"He's in last, in the black and yellow," she says.

His position didn't matter to me. I was just excited to see my dad.

Even then, I knew I wanted to get in on the action. My first bike was a Honda 50 minibike. To teach my brother and me to ride, my father put us in a ditch with our bikes and tied a rope around us. He held on to the other end and walked beside us. If we got scared and accidentally twisted the throttle too far, he'd yank us off the bikes before we got hurt. He always made us wear helmets and told us to never go riding alone.

When my father would crash and hurt himself during a jump attempt, he'd call us kids into the ambulance with him. "Look at me," he'd say to us. "Promise me you won't do what I do." Of the four of us kids, I was the one he disciplined the most, the one constantly challenging him—and emulating him. Pretty soon I was putting up a sign on our gate reading "See Evel Knievel Junior jump for 25 cents." Then I'd jump my minibike over ten bicycles.

My dad would flip out when I'd tear up my knees or break my arm riding in the mountains near Butte, Montana, where we lived. But once he realized that I wasn't going to stop, he decided to put me in his show so he could watch over me. It was great. At age eight, in 1971, I performed with him for the first time at Madison Square Garden, doing wheelie shows before his big jumps. Soon I had my own action figure as part of the Evel Knievel toy line. My dad and I traveled all over the United States, as well as to Australia. Beginning when I was fourteen or so, he'd let me drive his sixty-two-foot "Big Red" flatbed trailer, which had his name on the side and was filled with his bikes and touring equipment. We'd rumble down the highway as truckers would call out over the CB radio, "There goes Evel!"

But the good times didn't last. As a teenager, I argued a lot with my dad and got in some trouble, and at age nineteen, I moved out and embarked on my solo career as a daredevil. My dad struggled with the idea; he saw me as one of the many competitors who were trying to outjump him, but in reality, I was his biggest fan. Even during our time apart, his lessons stayed with me. Before one of my first big jumps, I became so anxious that I developed a fever, but then I remembered what he always told me: "It's normal for you to be nervous," he'd say, adding, "The bigger the crowd, the better you'll do."

He'd hear from folks about how good I had become, but that never stopped him from worrying about me. When we'd talk on the phone, he'd ask me, "Are you using a safety deck?" He'd seen other guys emulate him and end up paralyzed or killed, and I think he worried that if that ever happened to me, it would be on him.

In 1989, when I jumped the Caesars Palace fountains that he'd failed to clear in his attempt twenty-two years earlier, he was there with me. When I made it and said, "That was for you, Dad," I had never seen him so emotional.

After that, he supported my career. Now he was the one who'd pump up the crowds with wheelie shows before my big stunts. I went on to jump between two thirteen-story buildings, over an oncoming locomotive, even over the Grand Canyon. In the end, I did many more jumps than my father ever did. Like him, I suffered numerous broken bones, many difficult surgeries, and several crushed vertebrae. I'm lucky I'm still able to walk.

During the last few years of my father's life, he and I spent a lot of time together. We reminisced about the crazy lives we'd lived, and how lucky we'd been time and time again. I'd say to him, "I love you, Dad," and he'd tell me, "I love you, too, Rob."

Robert Edward Knievel III, aka Kaptain Robbie Knievel, is a stunt performer, daredevil, and author of the autobiography *Knievelution: Son of Evel.* He lives on the road and has two daughters.

My Father the Decathlete

Caitlyn Jenner

by *Brandon Jenner*

Caitlyn Jenner is a former Olympian and reality television star. Born William Bruce Jenner in Mount Kisco, New York, in 1949, Jenner was the breakout star of the 1976 Summer Olympics, where he won the men's decathlon and was dubbed "the world's greatest athlete." Following his retirement from sports, Jenner became a businessman and entrepreneur. He was married three times, most recently to Kris Jenner, with whom he starred in Keeping Up With the Kardashians. *In 2015, Jenner came out as a transgender woman and changed her name to Caitlyn. She has six children, Burt, Casey, Brandon, Brody, Kendall, and Kylie.*

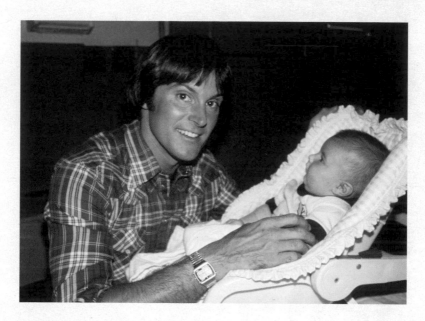

Bruce (now Caitlyn) and Brandon, 1981

M Y FATHER spent the first sixty-five years of her life trying to avoid answering the question "How are you doing?" And because of that, she didn't ask it often, either. And though I understand that she avoided the question because the answer would have laid bare too many struggles, it made my relationship with her challenging. People connect with each other through vulnerability, and you can only get someone to open up to you if you are willing to be vulnerable yourself. Because she was shielding something so important from herself, Dad remained distant for much of my life.

I am my mother's first child and my father's third. My half brother, Burt, and half sister Casey lived with their mother. My younger brother, Brody, my mother, my father, and I lived in a quaint wooden craftsman house in Malibu, one of the first built. But I don't have many memories from before my parents split up and my father moved out. I was four years old at the time. They got divorced because my dad had decided to start transitioning to female (at least that was what they had discussed). I, of course, was too young then to have any idea what was behind their decision.

I do, however, remember a few details from my early childhood that only made sense much later. For instance, when I was very young, I used to love to fiddle with people's ears. Once when I reached out to touch my dad's ears, he said, "Don't do that. I just had surgery." He pointed to a thin line of small black stitches behind his ear, grinned, and said, "They took my ear off, peeled my face back, and then stitched it back on." And a little while after my parents had divorced, I asked Mom what the deal was with Dad's boobs. She told me that sometimes when a man is muscular and then doesn't work out, he gets boobs. In reality, my father had had plastic surgery, was undergoing electrolysis, and was taking hormones in order to appear more feminine.

Though both of my parents did a good job of shielding my brother and me from their marital problems, I knew they were going through a difficult time. It was very confusing for my mother, and for my father as well. They went to therapy before ultimately deciding to divorce, and for the first few years after that, they were very amicable. Mom started dating David Foster, whom she later married. I never called him dad, but he was the one who lived with us, who told me to pick up my clothes and turn off the lights—all the typical dad things. So even though this essay is about Caitlyn, I could write one just as easily about David. He was a wonderful father figure.

A few years after my parents divorced, Dad apparently decided that it wasn't the right time to transition and had many of his surgeries reversed. After that, his relationship with my mother grew more hostile. She had worked hard to accept that the reason my dad couldn't be with her was because he was working toward transitioning. When he started dating Kris Kardashian, whom he would go on to marry, that line of reasoning fell apart. It was tremendously painful. The effect of my parents' souring relationship was that I didn't see my father more than half a dozen times between ages eight and twenty-five. Sadly, the infrequent exchanges felt more like staged photo opportunities than real bonding. In fact, they *were* staged photo ops for "family" Christmas cards: me, Brody, Burt, and Casey alongside our father. We were one big happy family. For a day.

Because of this, most of the memories I have of my dad are from the narrow slice of time before I was eight years old. I remember him betting Brody and me twenty dollars that he could beat us to the top of these insanely high sand dunes off the Pacific Coast Highway in Malibu and then just *smoking* us. He ran a flat-out decathlete sprint. He didn't even pretend to let us win.

Another time, he bought me a bike but made me promise I'd pay him back for it. It cost $250. Weeks later, we were at the beach together and Dad picked up an apricot off the ground. He pointed out a skinny little tree maybe fifty or sixty feet away. "Brandon," he said, "if you nail the trunk of the tree, you'll only owe me half for that bike." I was pitching Little League at the time, and, sure enough, I hit the tree. I was really proud of myself and thought he would be, too. Perhaps he was, but all he said was, "Now you just owe me one hundred twenty-five dollars." I was eight and had no idea how I'd make the money.

After Dad met and married Kris, family became a business for him, and I stayed away for most of my teenage years. I didn't want to be a part of their dynamic. I know now, though, that Dad was pretty unhappy in that house and felt he wasn't treated well.

When I was in my twenties and his daughters with Kris, Kendall and Kylie, were teenagers, my dad and I began to reestablish a relationship. Dad wasn't as needed around the house and, I think, was looking for someone to talk to. Although, to be honest, instead of talking, we *did* things. We worked on my 1965 Mustang Fastback or flew RC planes in the park near his house. But even then, it always seemed Dad had his guard up.

Once Dad decided to go through with the transition, I was the first of her children she confided in. My mother had told me what was going on a few years earlier, but I had never broached the subject with my father. As soon as Dad said it herself, I was so happy for her. It was as if she were truly stepping into who she was. I was proud, too, that she was publicly embracing something she had struggled with for so long. As her son, I wish my dad had been able to transition sooner, not only because I think she would have been happier, but because I think we could have built a stronger relationship earlier. Now I'm making up for lost time. I speak to my dad almost every day, and every time, she asks me, "How are you doing?"

Brandon Jenner is a singer and songwriter. He lives in Los Angeles, California, and has one daughter.

My Father the Dragon

Bruce Lee

by Shannon Lee

Bruce Lee is arguably the world's most famous martial artist. Born Lee Jun-fan in San Francisco, California, in 1940, Lee grew up in Kowloon, Hong Kong, where he began training in the martial arts to test his skills and defend himself against gang violence before moving back to the United States at age eighteen. As an actor, producer, and director, Lee starred in and created legendary films such as The Big Boss, Fist of Fury, Way of the Dragon, *and* Enter the Dragon. *He and his wife, Linda Emery, had two children, Brandon and Shannon. Lee died in 1973 at age thirty-two.*

I WAS ONLY FOUR YEARS OLD when my father died. We were in Hong Kong. I don't remember exactly where I was or how I found out, but I believe that my brother, Brandon, and I were with our mom at our home in Kowloon Tong when we got the news that our dad had been rushed to the hospital.

Accounts of my father abound, and I am careful to separate what memories are authentically mine from what I have learned through stories. All my very early memories are of Hong Kong, where we moved when I was two years old and lived until my father died two years later.

The greatest and most vivid memory I hold of my father is an overwhelming sense of being loved by him. That hasn't diminished in the years since he died. Throughout my life, I've always felt that I knew my father, that I had a sense of who he was as a human being and what was important to him energetically. I used to think I must be crazy to feel I knew this, given that we spent so little time together and I have so few memories of him. How could I have any idea what he might have wanted? But the thing about my dad, the thing you can see watching films of his even now, is how much of a presence he was. He wouldn't have said he was a master of life force, or "qi," but plainly he was. He could summon and deploy energy at will. His energy still pops off the screen directly into us. That is the power that so engraved itself upon my memory. That deep sense of being loved, of being supported, and of having confidence was instilled in me at a young age. I feel it holding me in my approach to the world and how I move through it. I feel safe. At certain times, this sense can become obscured, but it's always there when I really need it, reminding me who I am. My father hasn't been in my life since I was a toddler, but he's never stopped guiding me.

Martial arts has always been a part of our lives. Baba ("Dad" in Chinese) had turned our backyard into an informal Jeet Kune Do training ground. Guys like James Coburn, Chuck Norris, and Steve McQueen, as well as Baba's regular students like Ted Wong, Richard Bustillo, and Dan Inosanto, used to come over to train. I remember my mom telling me the story of Brandon's best friend, Luke, who never wanted to come over to our house because, as he said, "There are always grown men beating the crap out of each other in the backyard!"

After our father died, Brandon and I didn't study martial arts for many, many years. I tried, briefly, when I was about nine years old, taking a few Jeet Kune Do lessons with one of Baba's former students. But the pressure was too great without him. There was a lot of judgment and grief—all mine, but there nonetheless. In my twenties, I finally felt that the time was right, and I asked Ted Wong, who was a family friend, to teach me. I wanted to get closer to my father through his love of kung fu and the art he created.

Ted was my dad's protégé in that he had come to my father as a "blank slate," never having trained prior to working with him. After my father died, Ted pored over his writings, trying to connect the dots between what he had learned and what my father had left behind. Following Baba's lead, he had turned his backyard into an informal training area as well. Ted had gotten hold of a chunk of titanium, which he punched to toughen up his hands in the same way my father had used canvas bags and other materials to toughen his years before. Though this was in the early '90s, in Ted's backyard in Monterey Park, it felt like the '70s. There, under his guidance, I reconnected with my father through the movement art he had created.

My father was famous for saying, "Be like water," by which he meant to be fluid, responsive to the situation, alive, present. His Jeet Kune Do is a very simple art—there are no set forms and very few moves—but it requires great skill. Once you achieve a basic understanding, it's about being able to hone, adapt, and develop your second nature as a fighter. To practice Jeet Kune Do is to practice being alive, and in learning the art, I felt drawn even closer to my father.

Shannon (one year old) and Bruce in Los Angeles,
California, 1970

As I got older, I started to read more of my father's writings. Though they were usually about martial arts and Jeet Kune Do, they also made it clear that to be like water constituted an entire life philosophy. It's a philosophy of being open to the world, a philosophy of fluidity, and of being comfortable in the flux. Baba's words have been a tremendous comfort and inspiration to me in the ebb and flow of my own life. When Brandon died in 1993, I leaned heavily on my dad's writings to help me process that grief. Now, as a parent myself, I return again and again to my father's words. I am older than he ever got to be, but he is still guiding me. It's as if he has returned to me. It's as if he never left.

Shannon Lee is a writer, producer, actor, and speaker, and the founder and CEO of the Bruce Lee Family Companies and the Bruce Lee Foundation. She lives in Los Angeles, California, with her daughter.

My Father the Drug Lord Pablo Escobar

by Sebastián Marroquín

Pablo Escobar, one of the world's most infamous criminals, was born
in Rionegro, Colombia, in 1949. At the height of his power in the 1980s,
Escobar and his Medellín Cartel exported more than fifteen tons of cocaine,
accounting for more than 80 percent of the drug entering the United States.
His empire was fueled by violence, including a deadly siege on Colombia's
Supreme Court and the murders of politicians, police officers, judges, and
hundreds of civilians. Escobar and his wife, Victoria Eugenia Henao, had
two children, Sebastián Marroquín (born Juan Pablo Escobar Henao) and
Manuela. He died in 1993, in a shoot-out with a vigilante group named
Los Pepes, a day after his forty-fourth birthday.

Sebastián (age five) and Pablo, 1982

W HEN I WAS SEVEN YEARS OLD, outside a safe house in Panama City, Panama, my father turned to me and asked, "Do you know what a bandit is?" I nodded. He said, "I am a bandit. That's what I do for a living." He had just ordered the murder of Rodrigo Lara, Colombia's Minister of Justice. To have the minister killed was a big decision, since in doing so, my father would be publicly acknowledging that he was an outlaw. But he always knew what he was—a drug kingpin—and he never hid it from me.

I want to say, up front, that my father is 100 percent responsible for his crimes. But also that he was a wonderful father, one of the best in the world. Having a son myself now, I can see that. My earliest and happiest memories are of playing soccer with my dad at our home in Medellín and of the entire family gathering around the table for big meals. My father and I were very close friends. Everything changed for our family with the murder of Lara. Immediately my mother, sister, and I went into hiding in Panama, and my dad was rarely with us. The authorities were hunting for us all. Unlike what you see in popular depictions of that time, our lifestyle was not at all luxurious. We stayed in dingy and dirty homes. I was only seven, but I remember thinking, *What's the use of all my father's money if he still has to live like this?* You could be very rich, but you have to live like the poorest man in the world. It seemed so pointless.

Even when things were very grim, my dad was always near us. He called us and sent letters and recorded tapes for me and my sister, telling us stories. And we did see him, even when we were on the run. When I was eight years old, for instance, he sat me down and told me about drugs. By that time, my father was moving mostly cocaine, a lot of it. It was the biggest business in the world. He said, "A great man is the one who doesn't do drugs." The only drug he had tried was marijuana. But he knew I was surrounded by drugs and that all my friends had tried them. So he said, "When you become curious about them, just call me and we will do them together."

When I was a teenager, I did my best to persuade him to change. I told him if you have to defend your ideas with guns, you have to check your ideas. I told him I was tired of the violence, tired of watching my family and friends disappear. There had been numerous kidnapping attempts against me. I had barely survived a car bomb in 1988. There was just so much blood being spilled in Colombia, you can't imagine. I told my father he was the only person who could stop it. But he never listened to anyone—not the authorities and not his family. So I was shocked when he finally surrendered to the Colombian government in 1991 at La Catedral prison in Medellín and made a speech dedicating his surrender to his fourteen-year-old pacifist son. Unfortunately, it turned out he couldn't stop the violence or control his own violent nature. While in prison, he tortured and killed two of his lieutenants and shortly thereafter escaped and went back on the run.

I was sixteen years old when my father died. He committed suicide rather than be captured. I spoke to him ten minutes before it happened. He said, "I'll call you later." That was the last time I heard his voice. I didn't know he was dead until a journalist told me, live on television. I went crazy. I threatened the country and said that if my father was truly dead, I would kill everybody. Of course, I regret those words now. It breaks my heart that I will be remembered more for those five seconds of threats, from a son still in shock over the death of his father, than for the twenty-five years of peace that followed them.

Now I speak about my father's legacy in an attempt to prevent more carnage and violence. Sadly, the world has more Pablo Escobars than ever. But I am trying to leave a better future for my son than the one I inherited from my father. At the same time, my dad was very clever and full of love for me, my sister, and my mom. So in that sense I am trying to imitate him, but only the good parts.

Sebastián Marroquín is an architect in Buenos Aires, Argentina. His book, *Pablo Escobar: My Father*, was published in 2016.

My Father the Dude

Jeff Bridges

by Isabelle Bridges Boesch

Jeff Bridges is an actor, painter, singer, photographer, and producer.
Bridges, who comes from a prominent acting family, was born in
Los Angeles, California, in 1949. He began his acting career with his
father, Lloyd, in the series Sea Hunt *and went on to star in films*
such as The Last Picture Show, Fat City, Heaven's Gate, Tron, *and*
Crazy Heart, *for which he won an Oscar. He is perhaps best known*
for his role as the Dude in the Coen brothers film The Big Lebowski.
He is married to Susan Geston, and they have three daughters, Isabelle,
Jessica, and Haley.

Jeff with his daughters (from left to right), Hayley (eight years old), Jessica (ten years old), and Isabelle (twelve years old), on set in Los Angeles, 1993

M Y DAD CAME FROM A FAMILY OF ACTORS. His father, Lloyd, was an actor. His mother, Dorothy, was an actor. His brother Beau is an actor, too. He knows firsthand how weird and challenging it can be to have an actor as a parent, which means he is very good at *being* a famous actor father.

When I was growing up, my dad was really hitting his stride. He made many of his greatest films, from *The Fabulous Baker Boys* to *The Fisher King* to *Fearless*, before I was ten years old. He was often away shooting for weeks at a time, leaving my mother to look after me and my two sisters. She likes to say she takes care of the empire—and she does.

But when my dad was at home, it was like having the greatest, most imaginative friend in the world. What makes him such a wonderful actor is the same thing that makes him a wonderful playmate: he's a great pretender. He relished opening up his rich inner life to share with me and my sisters, and he was always happy to be part of ours, too. My sisters and I loved to dress him up, put flowers in his hair—he's always had a nice head of hair—and decorate his face with makeup. When Dad was around, we'd draw or paint or just play pretend for hours. He has such a playful spirit. The only time he ever brought his work home with him was the day he returned from shooting *Blown Away* still in makeup, his face appearing all bloodied and bruised. I think he wanted to scare us, but we just loved peeling off the stretchy plastic fake blood from his face. It was really satisfying.

But, of course, he couldn't always be at home. When he was away, Dad made sure we stayed connected. He'd call every night. He'd say something like, "Isabelle, when you're asleep tonight, you'll see a building. Go through the front door and climb up to the attic. What do you see?"

"I see the branch of an oak tree by the window," I'd reply.

Then he'd ask, "Do you see the tree house nestled in the crook of the branch?"

I'd laugh and say I did.

"Let's meet there tonight," he'd say. "What are we going to do?"

"We'll jump on our horses and ride to the mountains."

"Sounds like a plan," he'd say. In the morning, he'd call again, and we'd go over the adventures we'd had in our dreams the night before.

I always knew that my father was loving and sweet and playful, but it's still funny to me that he's become so closely identified with the Dude. By the time *The Big Lebowski* came out, I was in high school, and, just like a typical teenager, I had zero interest in my father's work. (I still haven't seen some of his films from that period.) What I remember most is that around that time, we were on vacation in Hawaii, and my dad was wearing those hideous Sun Jellies from the movie. They're one of the most well-known parts of his costume, but they were actually my dad's own shoes. Anyway, my sister and I were so embarrassed by those godawful jellies, we threw them into the ocean. Today, they'd probably be worth a lot of money. Another funny thing about people conflating Dad with the Dude is that he's not really a laid-back guy. He gets anxious. He experiences stress. Before he goes onstage, he always says he doesn't want to do it, and afterward, he is critical of himself. Though he describes himself as "Buddhish," and certainly those are themes reflected in the Dude, he doesn't project Zen calm.

He is, however, extremely present. Even more so now that he's older and a grandfather. I have two kids of my own, and he is very focused on being in their lives. We live in Oakland, but he and my mom visit often. And when he's not able to be with his grandkids, he calls to plan dream meetings with them, too.

Isabelle Bridges Boesch is a mother's empowerment coach and author. Her most recent book is *Daddy Daughter Day*, written with her father. She lives in Oakland, California, with her husband, daughter, and son.

My
Father
the
Duke
John
Wayne

by Ethan Wayne

Born Marion Robert Morrison in Winterset, Iowa, in 1907, John Wayne became synonymous with the American West through iconic roles in John Ford's Stagecoach, The Searchers, The Man Who Shot Liberty Valance, *and* True Grit. *Known as Duke, Wayne had an on-screen persona that was laconic, tough, and stoic. He had seven children, Michael, Mary Antonia, Patrick, Melinda, Aissa, Ethan, and Marisa.*

Ethan (age five) with John on the set of *El Dorado*, 1967

I WAS BORN IN 1962, at the height of my father's career. My father named me after Ethan Edwards, his character in *The Searchers*, which many critics consider to be his best role. Right after I was born, we moved from Los Angeles to Newport Beach, so my experience with my father is probably different from that of my much older half siblings.

My father was tough but very loving. He was old-school. I don't know how else to describe it. He didn't talk much, but he could make his few words very, very impactful and meaningful. Other actors fight for lines; my dad tried to remove as many words as possible. He learned from men who came before him—director John Ford, lawman Wyatt Earp (whom he had met while working as a prop boy), and silent film actor Harry Carey. When he first saw himself on-screen, he didn't like his voice, his look, the way he moved. He was very uncomfortable. So he figured out *that* guy walks right. *That* guy talks right. *This* guy acts like a man. He absorbed all of it from these people and built a persona called "John Wayne."

But his friends called him Duke, his childhood nickname. It was the name of his dog, an Airedale. Dad used to deliver papers with Duke. The local firemen called the pair Big Duke and Little Duke. The name stuck. He told me, "Now when someone calls me John, I don't even turn my head."

My dad was always thought of as a cowboy or a soldier-type. Strong, silent, stern. But in his free time, his life was centered on the ocean. We had a converted World War II minesweeper called *Wild Goose* that we used to motor out to the Channel Islands off the coast of Newport Beach. Every summer, we would sail up in British Columbia and Alaska. Every winter, we would take it down to Mexico, either to Baja or into the mainland.

When he wasn't on the boat, Dad was working. So I was raised on movie sets in places like Durango, Mexico; Ridgway, Colorado; and outside Santa Fe, New Mexico. Sets were rugged in those days. Our family would stay either in a small rented house or in a little motel. I had a tutor three hours a day, but I learned a lot from my father, too. He never told me "do this" or "do that" but led by example. You never wanted to disappoint him. Sometimes this meant being situationally aware on a set, not crossing into an eyeline, stepping into the frame, or making a sound when film was rolling.

Once when we were at a friend's ranch, he asked me to drive to the house in an old pickup truck and grab some things for him. I was twelve. I got the truck stuck, and I had to go tell him. He was in the middle of a card game. He didn't get up or offer to help. It was clear that I was expected to figure out how to get the truck out on my own.

Some of my proudest moments came from living up to my father's straight-ahead toughness. When we were in mainland Mexico, we'd anchor the boat far from the shore and swim in. It was about a twenty-five-minute swim. I remember once, when I was seven or eight years old, swimming into a bunch of sea snakes and saying, "Holy crap. There are sea snakes here, Dad!"

He replied, "Yeah, just keep swimming, kid."

Once we made it to shore, we walked around till our clothes dried. He gave me a big hug and said, "Good job, Big Stuff." I was just so proud to have made it through, proud to be my father's son.

My father died on June 11, 1979. I was seventeen. At the time, it was just him and me alone in the house; my mother had moved out. He had had lung cancer back in 1964, and it had recurred in his stomach. That day, he said he wasn't feeling well, so I drove him to UCLA. As we pulled up to the hospital, there was a crowd of photographers at the entrance waiting for him; I don't know who had tipped them off, but we had to go through the back. I was worried, but I was also a naive teenager and thought he was going to be okay. He just always got through things. I didn't know it at the time, but that was the last ride I would ever take with my dad.

Ethan Wayne is the chairman of the John Wayne Cancer Foundation and president of John Wayne Enterprises.

My Father the Dungeon Master

Gary Gygax

by Lucion Gygax

Ernest Gary Gygax, born in Chicago, Illinois, in 1938, was a game designer best known for creating Dungeons & Dragons with Dave Arneson in 1974. D&D went on to become the bestselling role-playing game in the world, with more than $1 billion in book and accessory sales and an estimated 20 million players. However, Gygax lost control of his company TSR, Inc., in 1985 and spent many years and his entire fortune trying to regain it. He had six children, Ernest Jr., Mary, Heidi, Cindy, Lucion, and Alexander. He died in 2008, at age seventy, having never regained control of TSR or his beloved game.

Gary and Lucion at GenCon (the largest tabletop-game convention in North America), in Indianapolis, Indiana, 2001

M Y FATHER WAS FIRED from his job as an insurance underwriter at Fireman's Fund on October 12, 1970. His newly promoted boss, Bruno, purposely picked that day because he knew it was my mother's birthday. To make matters worse, my mother was eight months pregnant with me, her fifth child. Bruno and my dad had been peers in the company, but Bruno didn't like my father because he was so good at the job that he would finish his work in half the time it took Bruno. Instead of doing the conventional thing and "looking busy," my dad would invite friends over during work hours to play war games. When Bruno got the promotion, he gleefully fired my dad to remove a potential rival. The ride back on the train from Chicago to Lake Geneva, Wisconsin, was long that day, as my father had to tell my mom that he was unemployed and they no longer had insurance coverage.

The silver lining was that my dad was entitled to unemployment payments. He discussed the situation with my mom and presented her with two options: they could move out of state so he could find another job in the insurance field (since Bruno had essentially blacklisted him with other firms in the Chicago area), or he could try to make it as an author. Moving would be difficult, as my parents were poor and neither had a driver's license. My mom supported his dream to become a writer and agreed to live on the meager unemployment checks as he gave it a go.

My father diligently banged away on his typewriter late into the night, and my mother endeavored to keep all of us quiet until noon so he could sleep. He completed a novel called *The Horn Bow* and sent it out to several publishers, only to receive rejection letter after rejection letter. Try as they might, my parents couldn't meet our family of seven's needs on unemployment. So my grandmother Almina, better known to me as Murmur, purchased all the machinery from a shoe-repair shop and paid for three weeks of cobbling lessons for my dad. She knew that her son was best suited to being his own boss.

This is how my father came to be a cobbler in Lake Geneva in 1973. The shoe-repair industry didn't pay well. Food was scarce. My mother gardened, canned vegetables, baked bread, and generally did her best to help us subsist. The elder children got their clothes from secondhand stores, and the younger ones wore hand-me-downs. Our life was difficult, so when a local businessman offered my twelve-year-old brother, Ernie, a job as a shoeshine boy, my parents agreed to let him accept it. Ernie enjoyed the work and brought home two hundred dollars in a week. My parents were stunned; they started asking questions about the job, and that's how they found out that Ernie was shining shoes at the Playboy Club. The money was fantastic, but they weren't going to let him work at such a place. Shortly thereafter, my parents swallowed their pride and applied for food stamps. With government aid, they were able to put enough food on the table to feed the family. This was the state of the Gygax family when my dad created Dungeons & Dragons.

The way it happened is this: Through some fellow gamers, my father was introduced to Dave Arneson, who had developed a new twist on fantasy miniature gaming. My dad invited Arneson to Lake Geneva and had him run a session. Immediately Dad saw the potential in this idea and how it could be, pardon my pun, a game changer. There wasn't a rule set developed yet, so he began working on a way to translate this concept into words so that others could create their own fantastic adventures.

Dad took these components, Arneson's rough concept, and decades of science fiction and fantasy reading and started crafting what would come to be known as Dungeons & Dragons. His excitement about this new game was boundless. But when he took it to game publishers, they all passed.

That didn't deter him. Dad was all in. He was convinced that D&D would usher in a new era of gaming. But how could he bring this wonderful new game to the market? He was a cobbler barely able to provide for his young family. Finally, his lifelong friend Don

Kaye agreed to help him out. Don was a machinist and didn't have much money, either, but he cashed in a life insurance policy to get one thousand dollars, enough to start Tactical Studies Rules, the company that would publish the three core rules volumes for D&D: *Men & Magic*, *Monsters & Treasure*, and *The Underworld & Wilderness Adventures*.

The game came out in 1974, and its popularity built slowly at first, then more rapidly. My father's instincts were right, and the future looked bright. This was the beginning of a radical change for my family. Suddenly we had money. Dad went from being that poor guy with long hair to a respected entrepreneur.

After years of renting, we finally bought a house. But the thing I remember most about our change of fortune was going to the grocery store. "Can we have this cereal?" one of us kids would ask, pointing to a name-brand box like King Vitaman or Cap'n Crunch, and for the first time that we could remember, Mom said yes.

For a while, things were idyllic. But in the 1980s, everything began to sour. The new investors Dad brought in after Don Kaye died, tragically, in 1976, had gotten the company in financial trouble despite record sales of D&D. During this time, my parents filed for divorce and began a protracted and contentious battle that lasted several years. Dad moved out to Los Angeles to try to get a D&D movie made. He succeeded in getting a D&D cartoon on the air, but he was never able to get the movie into development. He was splitting his time between Lake Geneva and LA, trying to manage both aspects of the company as well as he could.

That would change in 1985, when, after a bitter dispute, my dad was removed as chairman from the company he had founded. Dungeons & Dragons and all the intellectual property he had created were held by the company. He had started TSR with his close friend and never envisioned a hostile stock takeover. Dad would go on to spend all the money he had trying to get the company back, but he was never able to prove his case in court. In a few short years, we went from being financially comfortable to once again being poor. I graduated valedictorian of my class in 1988 and headed off to college at the University of Wisconsin–Madison. However, my family didn't have money to send me back for my sophomore year. I decided to join the army to pay my own way through college when I got out, and that's what I did. I told Dad after I'd already enlisted. He was against it, but I think he understood and eventually was proud of my decision.

That was in 1989. I have served continuously since then, both on active duty and as a reservist. Currently I am serving on active duty as the operations officer for the 224th Sustainment Brigade in the California Army National Guard. I've served two tours in Iraq and earned a Combat Infantryman's Badge, a Bronze Star, and numerous other awards. I found that all the role-playing games I played with my dad served me well in my career as a soldier. I practiced many skills at the gaming table and didn't even realize it until much later. I learned how to improvise, to problem-solve, to influence others, to read small-group dynamics, and to speak persuasively. Those were skills I learned not only from playing games with my dad but also through watching how steadfast he remained, navigating the twists and turns, the peaks and valleys of his life, eye always steady on the horizon.

Lucion Gygax is the operations officer for the 224th Sustainment Brigade as well as the CEO of Gary Con Gaming Convention, a memorial gathering held in honor of his father every March in his hometown of Lake Geneva, Wisconsin. He resides in Calabasas, California, with his wife and their three daughters.

My Father the Executioner

Donald A. Cabana

by Kristin Fitzgerald

Donald A. Cabana was born Dominic Arturo Spinelli in Lowell, Massachusetts, in 1945, and entered the foster care system soon after. He was adopted by Samuel and Dorothy Cabana and chose to change his name at ten years old. He and his wife, Miriam Sue Ables, had six children, Scott, Michelle, Ashley, Angela, Christopher, and Kristin. He served as a warden for several prisons around the United States. After presiding over multiple executions, Cabana became a passionate opponent of the death penalty, as chronicled in his memoir, Death at Midnight: The Confession of an Executioner. He died in 2013, at age sixty-seven.

Donald with five-month-old Kristin (right) and her twin brother, Christopher, at their house at the Mississippi State Penitentiary, 1985

W E'D SIT ON THE BACK-PORCH SWING, just Dad and me, holding hands, rocking back and forth after dinner while he quizzed me on our favorite subjects.

"What's the capital of Vermont?"

"In what year did the Salem Witch Trials take place?"

"Who was the last baseball player to hit .400?"

As an eight-year-old with five siblings, I cherished those moments between the two of us. My dad had just finished his career as a prison warden, and we had moved to Hattiesburg, Mississippi, where he had begun working on his PhD in adult education at the University of Southern Mississippi. Whereas when he was a warden, my twin brother and I had played in large prison conference rooms, we now spent hours running up and down the steep, narrow staircase that led to his office in McCleskey Hall, a crumbling relic of 1930s building codes.

Even then, as a doctoral candidate, he began to lecture at Harvard, Cambridge, and Yale. We regularly answered phone calls at our home from *Dateline* and the *Today* show. A German film crew came to our house to make a documentary, and Chris Cuomo arrived in our tiny town to interview both of my parents for *20/20*. I remember that last incident well, because my mother made us clean our kitchen meticulously for days beforehand, terrified that the tiniest speck of dirt or grime might appear in the background on national television. The media sought my father's opinion as one of the few "death penalty experts" in the United States, as he had presided over two executions at the Mississippi State Penitentiary as warden and participated in others in Missouri and Florida. He spoke out unabashedly against the practice, becoming a somber voice of experience within the anti–death penalty community.

To me and my siblings, though, he was simply Dad. We teased him about every interview, knowing that the man we saw looking so professional and serious on television came home and played made-up games like "Just the Daughters, Not the Sons" and "Park Bench." (The premises and the rules changed every time we played.) All six of us spent countless hours trying to free ourselves from headlocks, noogies, and games in which my dad could use his considerable strength against us.

He taught us to both cheer and curse the Red Sox, swearing at their every mistake. The Yankees, though, particularly Derek Jeter, were the subject of his most vociferous baseball-fueled outbursts. To quote one of Dad's favorite movie characters, Ralphie from *A Christmas Story*, my father "worked in profanity the way other artists might work in oils or clay. It was his true medium." He also applied his medium to burned food, bad drivers, and my brothers.

Dad didn't ever lecture us about the death penalty or his thoughts on the justice system. We spent most nights simply talking around the dinner table with him and my mom, whose conversations with us and with each other served as teaching enough. In fact, most of the time when Dad held court at the dinner table, we ended up rolling around laughing. We'd start talking about the news or someone at school, and somehow or another it would remind him of a funny anecdote. Dad had a great sense of humor and also a knack for using different voices and mannerisms to bring these experiences to life; he was the consummate storyteller.

Amid the laughter, there were moments of seriousness, such as when he brought his profession home with him. He returned to the Mississippi State Penitentiary when I was in college, and later served as warden in a regional jail closer to Hattiesburg. Sometimes, after an incident at work, he would stare off into space and muse, almost to the wall instead of any one person, about how he couldn't understand some of the people he worked with, inmates and prison officials alike. Those who didn't feel empathy. Those who abused children or murdered in cold blood. Those who lorded their authority over others.

For the most part, however, he was as optimistic as anyone in his profession could be. His Catholic faith remained important to him throughout his life, buoying his spirit and giving him a perspective all too often disregarded in his line of work. He believed that people can and do change. For him, that included inmates, whom he felt had been entrusted to his care. Perhaps the most poignant evidence of this belief came after he died. When my brother and I cleaned out Dad's office, amid his boxes of awards and honors, we found numerous poems, letters, and illustrations inmates had given to him throughout his career. They thanked him for treating them with respect. For giving them hope. For helping them change.

My memories of my father, in the years after his death, don't revolve around his accolades. Like all who knew him, I remember most how he made me feel: loved. In my mind, Dad isn't standing behind a podium, giving a speech. Nor is he walking the halls, checking prison cells. For me, Dad is still sitting on that back-porch swing after dinner, holding my hand and asking questions.

Kristin Fitzgerald is a stay-at-home parent and a small-business owner. She lives in Nashville, Tennessee, with her husband and three children.

My Father the Farmer

Wendell Berry

by Mary Berry

Wendell Berry is an author, poet, activist, essayist, and farmer. He was born in Henry County, Kentucky, in 1934 and has written more than forty books, including novels, collections of poetry, and his seminal work, The Unsettling of America: Culture and Agriculture. In 2010, he was awarded the National Humanities Medal by President Barack Obama. Berry lives with his wife, Tanya, in Port Royal, Kentucky, and has two children, Mary and Den.

I WAS BORN IN LEXINGTON, KENTUCKY (not too far from where I live now), but for much of my childhood, my family lived all around the world. When I was two years old, in 1960, we moved to Mill Valley, California, where Daddy spent the year on a writing fellowship at Stanford University. We then returned to Henry County, Kentucky, and spent a year at the Home Place, the farm where my grandfather and great-grandfather had been born. Then my father got a Guggenheim Fellowship that allowed us to move to Europe for a year. My most vivid memories of that period are of our time in a little stone house in Fiesole, just north of Florence, where we lived for six months. I remember my mother cutting doll clothes out of paper bags and Daddy working at his Royal Crown typewriter. When the fellowship was over, we moved to New York City for a time—Daddy taught at NYU—and we lived in what is now Tribeca, in a loft outfitted with a swing and a trapeze. I loved it.

In 1963, my father was offered a job teaching English at the University of Kentucky. We moved to Lexington and bought a small farm in Henry County as a weekend place. It was my city-born mother who encouraged him to return to Henry County, then made a home for them on that farm, which they've now lived on for fifty-five years. Up until that point, no one of influence in my father's life had said he could be a writer and live in Henry County, except for his family. In fact, he was told that leaving New York would ruin his literary career.

During all that moving around when I was young, I wasn't miserable, but I was homesick for Kentucky. I used to play Flatt & Scruggs records and cry for home. My great-grandfather, when he got back from the one and only trip he ever took in his life, said that he had seen nothing he liked better than the field behind his barn. Like my grandfather and my father, I am his heir in that sentiment.

Daddy is a born teacher. He was always pointing out to my brother and me how a farmer plowed his field or what he'd done with his hay. He taught us that farming was a high calling and that a *good* farmer must have an incredible amount of sense, intelligence, and cultural knowledge. Daddy has a practice of splitting his day between working outside and writing. When I was young, he wanted my brother and me to work with him, and there was plenty to do: rocks to pick up, fences to mend, trees to prune, neighbors to help. I was grumpy as hell about it. Nevertheless, I grew up believing there were only three ways to make a decent living: to be a farmer, to be a writer, or to be a lawyer (like my grandfather and uncle).

I never really disagreed with my father. But in my teens, I did just want to be a regular Henry County Kentuckian. My parents had no interest in that. They demonstrated against war, against dams, against airports. We drove a VW camper van whereas most of our neighbors had pickup trucks. Author and Merry Prankster Ken Kesey, a dear friend of my father's, would come by with his hippie friends. When we put a composting privy in when I was thirteen or fourteen, I thought it was the biggest humiliation that could happen to a young person. My father used the compost to fertilize the tomatoes, and when my dates would come pick me up, he would point out the volunteer tomato plants and say, "Mary ate that tomato." My father was well-known enough then that he was frequently interviewed, and during interviews, he talked often of the toilet. We must have had the most famous bathroom in the state of Kentucky.

My father and mother have lived interesting, useful, beautiful lives full of friends from around the world—and our dear Henry County neighbors, too. My father made sure I understood that the importance of the arts of farming, gardening, and cooking was equal to that of the "high" arts of writing, painting, and music. I was fully grown before I heard anyone called "just a farmer."

I'm sure Daddy could have continued to travel around the world. But the greatest gift he gave to me was coming home.

Mary Berry is the executive director of the Berry Center. She is married to a farmer and lives in Henry County, Kentucky.

Mary (age three) with Wendell on their farm near Port Royal,
Kentucky, 1961

My Father the Father

Thomas S. Sullivan

by Jim Graham

Thomas S. Sullivan was one of the thousands of priests in the Catholic Church who has had a child. Sullivan, born in 1908 in New Bedford, Massachusetts, was working in a parish in Buffalo, New York, when he had an affair that ultimately led to the birth of a son, Jim Graham. Jim never met his father, who died in 1993 at age eighty-five.

I GREW UP IN A SMALL HOUSE—just one floor, with a basement and an attic—in a lower-middle-class neighborhood thirty minutes from downtown Buffalo. There were a lot of people in that house: John Graham, the man I called "Dad"; his sister, Kathryn; their parents, Stella and Otto Graham; and me and my two sisters, Joan and Connie.

I thought this was my family. Stella held us all together. She cooked, cleaned, cut the grass, did everything. She didn't say much; she just worked. Dad ran a gas station in Buffalo. I lived with the Grahams until I was eighteen, when I moved to New York City. Their home was a depressing place. My sisters and I took to calling ourselves the Grims.

My dad did not like me and treated me poorly. He was a burly, gruff, rough guy, and I was afraid of him. We barely spoke. There were no pictures of our mother in the house. It was just understood that we didn't talk about her or communicate with her. At the age of six, I got up enough courage to ask Dad what I should tell my friends who kept asking me about my mother. "Tell them she's dead," he said. She wasn't.

I knew I had a mother because she'd send me beautiful Christmas packages and birthday cards. And I would see her twice a year, when she would visit for four consecutive days at Eastertime and in August. She could only see my sisters and me between 10:00 a.m. and 7:00 p.m., at Dad's discretion. No overnights. She would pull up in front of the house, and my sisters and I would pile into her car to spend the day with her. When she and my father had gotten divorced, he had retained custody of us. When I asked my mother why, she explained that he had hired a powerful attorney. I came to find out that wasn't exactly true. There *was* a powerful attorney—the legendary William Mahoney, head of the local Democratic Party in Erie County, New York, who had defended many high-profile clients, including members of the mafia—but my dad hadn't hired him. The Catholic Church had.

I was forty-eight years old when I finally learned the truth of who my real father was. This was 1993, a full fourteen years after John Graham, the man who I thought was my father, had passed away and a month after my mother's death. I was out to dinner with my wife. The conversation turned to the Grahams, and I remarked that my relationship with them had been strained since my father's death.

"I'll tell you why that is," my wife said. "John wasn't your father. Father Sullivan was."

The secret had been revealed to her by John's brother, Otto Jr., who'd been annoyed with me for complaining about the way I had been raised and thought the news would upset me. My wife had asked around for confirmation and gotten it from the other family members. That, with the help of a little vodka over dinner, was enough to prompt her to tell me.

I later confronted the Grahams. They were stone-faced for a while, then Kathryn slid an obituary across the kitchen table. It was Father Sullivan's. "This man may have been your father, but only your mother, John, and Father Sullivan would know for sure, and they're all dead," Kathryn said. I peered at the photograph and the man staring back at me. I noticed the date. He had died just a few months earlier.

I desperately wanted to know more about this man, but the Church appeared determined to keep my parentage a secret. After a lot of detective work, however, I learned some of the details of my father's life. Father Thomas S. Sullivan had taught theology at the seminary at Holy Angels parish in Buffalo. That's where he met and started a relationship with my mother, who at the time was married to John, with whom she'd already had my sisters. Shortly after I was born, rumors started swirling throughout the parish that I looked more like Father Sullivan than I did John Graham. John was advised by the Church to move his family into his parents' home so his mother could ensure that Father Sullivan didn't come to visit me and my mother.

Jim (ten years old)

Father Sullivan, meanwhile, was transferred four hundred miles away to a church in Newburgh, New York. He disappeared from there a month later. Shortly after, my mother fled Buffalo with me, leaving my sisters behind, to meet up with him. They connected in Manhattan. My father had taken a job as a bartender and short-order cook and was living in an apartment on the West Side. My mother was living in the nurse's quarters of the hospital where she worked. They put me in the New York Foundling Hospital, an orphanage, and paid two dollars a day to the Sisters of Charity to take care of me. I was there for thirteen months. My mother came on her day off, once a week, to take me out. Often my father would be waiting up the block to take over pushing my baby carriage.

Then on July 29, 1947, a group made up of private detectives, John, his brother, and a family friend, Pat Sheehy, found my mother and Father Sullivan in bed together in his apartment during a midnight "raid." It was my second birthday. Once my father was found, the Church started the process of bringing him back into the fold. Despite his initial objections, he was sent to a rehabilitation camp in Essex, New York, called the Oblates of Mary Immaculate, where he spent sixteen years. Some priests referred to the facility as the Gulag, or Priest Prison. It's where wayward priests were sent to serve their "sentence."

The Church has never acknowledged that Sullivan was my father. However, on June 18, 2018, the day after Father's Day, I was able to exhume his body for DNA testing and confirm it. The Church still does not want to admit what they did seventy years ago. But DNA doesn't lie. My father was a priest, and the Church prevented me from knowing him. To me, Otto Jr.'s revelation, intended to be an act of retribution, was actually a gift. It was the key to solving all those childhood mysteries of why John was so cruel to me. Plus, had I not found out, my parents' story never would have been uncovered.

I've learned a lot about my father and myself during this process. He had had a domineering mother who pushed him to get straight A's and become the academic of the Oblate order. He had a quick wit. (Mine is the same.) My father had the same powerful voice I do. I have a booklet he wrote called "Our Lady of Hope" about an apparition of Mary in Pontmain, France, in 1871 that stopped a war. The booklet has been reprinted again and again. He was an eloquent writer. I know that not only from this pamphlet but from many of his letters, written to the General Superior in Rome during his time in the Gulag, asking to be reinstated with his full priestly rights. Though beautifully written, they are difficult for me to read, due to the subject matter.

I'm often asked what I have missed, not knowing my father. I wonder what it would have been like to be raised by him. He was a writer, a reader, a debater, an academic. My education would have been totally different. My father was all about higher learning. If I had had his mentoring, where would I have ended up? I'll never know, and that's a very painful answer. Nonetheless, I'm grateful that I finally verified the truth.

Jim Graham and his wife live in Seneca, South Carolina. Following a fifty-year career in sales and marketing, Jim is currently writing his memoir.

My Father the Hero

Walter Ehlers

by Catherine Metcalf

Walter Ehlers was born in 1921 in Junction City, Kansas. He joined the army in 1940 and took part in the D-Day invasion, landing on Omaha Beach on June 6, 1944. Three days later, after his unit came under fire, he distinguished himself in battle, single-handedly overtaking several German machine-gun nests and putting their crews out of action. Though injured, Ehlers refused treatment and returned to the field. He survived the war and was awarded the Congressional Medal of Honor. He and his wife, Dorothy, had three children, Catherine, Tracy, and Walter Jr. Ehlers died in 2014, at age ninety-two.

S OMETIMES THE EXPERIENCE OF WAR changes who a person is. Sometimes it simply reveals who they've been all along. My father entered the war a nineteen-year-old Kansas farm boy. He was tough; his family had already survived the Depression, battled bankruptcy, and faced starvation. So the actions of my father on June 9 and 10, 1944, for which he was awarded the Medal of Honor, did not so much define him as express who he already was, albeit in a deadly and dramatic context.

By the time I was born in 1956, my father had been out of the service for eleven years and had had the Medal of Honor for as long. He didn't hide it—the medal was displayed on the wall in our den—but he didn't talk about it much, either. What I knew in my early years about his time in the service I learned from climbing up on the sofa and reading the citation that accompanied the golden five-pointed-star-shaped medal, the official description of his actions on those two fateful days. Those were the first words I ever read. I taught myself how to sound out the opening lines, which I can still remember years later:

> For conspicuous gallantry and intrepidity at the risk of his life above and beyond the call of duty on 9–10 June 1944, near Goville, France. S/Sgt. Ehlers, always acting as the spearhead of the attack, repeatedly led his men against heavily defended enemy strong points exposing himself to deadly hostile fire whenever the situation required heroic and courageous leadership.

My father was just a regular dad. When I was growing up, he worked at the VA hospital in Long Beach, California, as a benefits counselor. He got to work at 8:00 a.m. and left at 5:00 p.m. We all had dinner together. He was involved in the Optimist Club and was a member of the Rotary Club. He wasn't ashamed of being a war hero, of course, but he didn't boast about it. What I recall most from the early years before my brother and sister were born was spending time with him in the garage, which he had turned into a woodshop. He had built deep shelves that lined the walls, and there was one that was the perfect size for a little girl, happy to be near her father, to nestle into with a book to read.

But sometimes the world outside would beckon Dad, like when the White House called to invite him to a reception in the Rose Garden, or to fly to France on Air Force One for the twentieth anniversary of D-Day. He was especially busy around patriotic holidays, like Memorial Day and Veterans Day, when he was often asked to ride in a parade. He used to take me along with him, so I'd put on my Easter dress and gloves and sit up on the back of a convertible, rolling down Ocean Boulevard in Long Beach. He'd happily participate in these events, but when they were over, he would unfasten the blue ribbon and place the Medal of Honor back in its frame on the wall. Dad lost his brother Roland on Omaha Beach, and he always believed that his brother was the one who deserved the recognition. "I was just doing my job," Dad said. "Those who made the ultimate sacrifice were the true heroes."

And that was that—the most I heard my father talk about the war for years. What I witnessed instead was his unflappable presence, a way of being in the world that carried with it supreme confidence. Nothing ruffled him. Whether this was because he had been through the war or that this quality had carried him through the war to begin with, I didn't know, nor did I, as a young girl, care. He made great waffles. He loved to roughhouse with our oversize German shepherd, Tippy Tin Tin, a relative of Hollywood's Rin Tin Tin. He taught me how to use a miter saw. We pulled weeds together in the yard. He had a quiet chuckle, not a loud laugh. He didn't raise his voice—he raised his eyebrows. When I had nightmares, I'd run into my parents' bedroom, and my father would comfort me. He loved my brother, my sister, and me absolutely and unconditionally.

In 1970, I was in middle school, studying world history. World War II had ended a quarter century before, and the country was again at war, this time in Vietnam. My father was deeply involved in

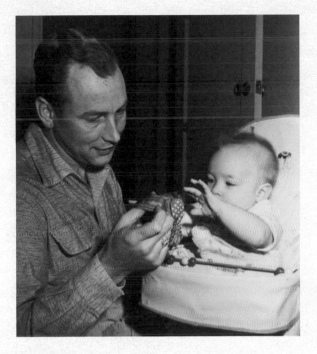

Walter showing Catherine (six months old) his medal at
their home in Buena Park, California, 1957

Veterans Affairs and still suffering from wounds incurred in France. In fact, he had just gone to the San Diego veterans hospital to have a piece of shrapnel removed from his shoulder. I took the shrapnel in to show my class. My teacher, Mr. Wilson, asked which war my father had fought in, and I told him World War II and said Dad was a Medal of Honor recipient. Mr. Wilson turned white with disbelief and asked if my father would talk to the class.

Dad agreed and a few days later took time off from his job to come in. I had read about my father's actions in the citation, and I knew he was a hero. But to hear him speak about Normandy in front of my class filled me with enormous pride. This was *my* dad. That day, he became a hero to all my friends, too.

I heard him speak about his experiences countless times after that. As the oldest surviving Medal of Honor recipient from Normandy, he was called upon increasingly in his later years to speak about his time in the service during World War II. His refrain never changed. He had been doing his job. His brother and the others who lost their lives on the battlefield were the real heroes.

When my father died in 2014, the 1st Infantry Division's 18th Infantry Regiment called to say they were sending a unit to do full military honors. General Wiggins, the commander of the US Army North, wanted to deliver a speech. Pete Wilson, the former governor of California and a dear friend of my father's, spoke as well. But what moved me most as we prepared for the funeral were my son Reed's words. He told me, "Mom, make sure they don't reduce Grandpa to just the Medal of Honor. He was so much more than those two days." For Reed and his brother and sister, my dad was the guy at Little League, at band concerts, at recitals, and at Scouts. He was the grandpa who took the kids to Disneyland on season passes. To me, he was a national hero, of course, but he was also, forever, Dad.

Catherine Metcalf taught English at Cal State Fullerton for thirty-three years. Currently she is the vice president of education at the Congressional Medal of Honor Society. She lives in Orange, California, and is a mother of three.

My Father the Hostage

Terry Anderson

by *Sulome Anderson*

Born in Lorain, Ohio, in 1947, Terry Anderson is a journalist and foreign correspondent. He has two daughters—Gabrielle with his first wife, Mihoko Anderson, and Sulome with his second wife, Madeleine Bassil. On March 16, 1985, while living in Beirut, Lebanon, and serving as the Middle East bureau chief for the Associated Press, he was kidnapped by a group associated with Hezbollah, becoming one of the 104 men and women held in the Lebanese Hostage Crisis from 1982 to 1992. Sulome was three months old when he was kidnapped. After being held for six years and nine months, he was released in 1991.

Terry with Sulome (six years old) in Damascus, Syria, following his release from captivity in 1991. This was their first meeting.

"I LIKED YOUR FATHER," says the man who held him hostage for nearly the first seven years of my life.

He sighs. He wants me to understand. "It was nothing personal," he tells me. "Our fight was not with him or the other hostages. Our fight was with the people who had slaughtered our families."

I am interviewing one of the guards who watched over my dad as he crouched, chained and blindfolded, on a series of dirty basement floors in Dahieh, a Shia suburb in south Beirut. This man is now a local Hezbollah official in south Lebanon, but at the time he held my father, he was just a teenage militiaman—pretty far down on the terrorist totem pole, as these things go.

Like my father was at the time of his kidnapping, I am now a journalist working in Beirut, and in a bizarre twist of fate, I've ended up face-to-face with one of his captors. To make matters even more complicated, the man seems very sorry about it.

"If I could go back in time, I would put you in your father's arms myself," he tells me.

I remember when I first felt my father's arms around me. It was the night he was released, at the US embassy in Damascus, Syria. They were stiff and unnatural, like an overstarched sweater. He was smiling from ear to ear, but his eyes were empty in a hollow face. My dad was finally home, but I instantly began mourning the loss of another father, the chubby, kind-eyed man whose photo I used to sleep with under my pillow—the person he was before they took him.

When I was nine, I snuck a copy of the memoir he wrote about his time in captivity into my room, where I read the whole thing in a day after being grounded following one of our daily screaming fights. My parents hadn't wanted me to read it, thinking I was too young, but I had to know more about this stranger-father and why he couldn't love me.

I learned a lot from that book. I found out why he called me "Button," a nickname I hated for the unnatural way he said it in the rare moments he showed me affection. The first time he saw me on TV, when his guards allowed him to watch the news, he thought my tiny nose looked just like a button. I cried as I read, wondering what was wrong with me that he could feel so much love from afar but not when I was living in the same house, not for the stubborn, hurt little girl who just wouldn't be quiet and do what she was told.

Every detail of his captivity—the torture, the agony, the casual cruelty of his kidnappers—was forever burned into my mind. I read that when his captors wouldn't let him send us a Christmas message one year, my father beat his head against the wall until he was covered in blood and they had to restrain him. They couldn't let him hurt himself too badly, after all. A dead hostage is no longer valuable. He wasn't even allowed the agency of suicide.

In the years after my dad came home, I would remember the time before he returned with a guilty nostalgia for which I hated myself. I was happy before he came barging into my life. I had been a bright, curious child, and the people around me had given me lots of attention and praise; I was the adorable little girl whose father was a hostage. I knew who I was back then.

When he first returned, I would tentatively try to share my thoughts and childlike discoveries with my new father, but unlike the adults who once cooed and exclaimed at my precociousness, he usually brushed me off. I knew almost immediately that he was jealous of my relationship with my mother, who had orbited me like a little moon from the moment of my birth. He was determined to make me less spoiled, as he saw it through the lens of his own upbringing. I realized later that when he would yell at me to sit still and stop being a smartass, his parents' words were coming out of his mouth.

By the time I was ten, I had become deeply, chronically insecure. My thoughts and feelings, which had once mattered, suddenly did not—at least to the one person I yearned for them to matter to. I began seeing myself as flawed and unwanted, the kind of gift you hope comes with a receipt. One day, I cut off my cloud of blond curls with a pair of craft scissors, trying to make myself look as ugly as I felt. Among my peers, I would adopt a similar interpersonal pattern as with my father, alternating between extreme vulnerability and an overaggressive demand to be noticed. My schoolmates smelled weakness, and I became a target for bullying, which only widened the fracture between the confident, assertive little girl I had been and the wounded preteen I was becoming.

That wound at my core would continue to fester for years, leading me into a spiral of pain and addiction that lasted well into adulthood. My father remained little more than an angry stranger for most of my life, and until recently, I would look in his eyes and see my deficiencies mirrored in his remoteness.

So two decades later, as the man who had taken the father I needed from me before I was born looks me in the eye and tells me he is sorry, I want to spit at him.

"You ruined my family," I tell him. "You nearly destroyed my life."

"What can I say, Susu?" he replies, pain etched across his face. "Your father is a good man, the best out of all those we took. But it could have been anyone. If someone else had caught our eye, we would have taken him. I look at you now and I feel for you. I think about your father and I feel for him, too. But at the time, we didn't see your father as Terry Anderson, the person. To us, he was America."

I think about the way the chasm between my father and me has diminished in recent years, as I begin to accept him for who he is and not who I always wished he could be. I hold the moments of closeness we've had next to my heart, the shared love of journalism, the increasing flashes of emotion and genuine affection he's shown me since he realized how much his trauma damaged my psyche.

My father's kidnapper is right. My dad is a good man. He may never have been the parent I longed for, but he has become something else to me, something just as precious and coveted. He is my friend now, and nobody can ever take that away from us again.

Sulome Anderson is a writer and journalist based in New York City and Beirut, Lebanon. Her most recent book is *The Hostage's Daughter: A Story of Family, Madness, and the Middle East.*

My Father the Hostage Negotiator Jack Cambria

by Melissa Cambria

As lead hostage negotiator for the New York Police Department, Jack Cambria participated in thousands of hostage crises. He's probably most well-known for John Turturro's fictionalized portrayal of him in the 2009 remake of The Taking of Pelham 123. *Over his thirty-three-year career with the NYPD, the Brooklyn, New York, native (born in Carroll Gardens in 1954) rose from beat cop to lieutenant in Sunset Park, headed up the Emergency Services Unit, and, finally, led the Hostage Negotiation Team. He currently provides hostage-negotiation training around the world and consults for film and television. He has two children, Melissa and Chris.*

T HE DAY I WAS BORN, my dad was up on the Brooklyn Bridge, talking a potential jumper down. He saved the guy and then rushed over to the hospital where my mother was in labor, sirens blaring. He made it in time.

During more than three decades with the NYPD, my dad conducted more than five thousand hostage negotiations. When it came to his children, he was, obviously, a tough cookie—I never really got away with the typical bargaining teenagers do. The rules were the rules. The thing is, though, Dad was almost preternaturally calm. He rarely got ruffled. I chalk this up, of course, to his professional training.

But most of Dad's approach—not only to his work but to us, his family—came from his Brooklyn upbringing. Dad was born in Carroll Gardens and grew up in Bensonhurst, two small family-oriented neighborhoods in New York City. He always had a sense of community. What's more, his parents raised him to treat everyone with the same level of respect. Respect was a big thing in the Cambria household. As Dad worked his way up from being a beat cop in Sunset Park to a SWAT team leader, these early lessons really helped him. He could connect with anyone. He got down—or up—to their level and spoke to them without judgment.

I think Dad was so tired of enforcing rules all day at work that at home, he just went along with whatever Mom said. He was also really easy to talk to. He had a saying he used at work and at home: "Always talk to me. Tell me what's going on." I was a good kid and didn't get into as much trouble as my friends. I made sure to always tell Dad how good I was, too.

But though Dad was calm, there were some lines we weren't to cross. I had a midnight curfew, which, by and large, I respected. But one night, a bunch of friends and I went to a nightclub out on Eighteenth Avenue in Bensonhurst. I meant to call my dad to tell him

I was going to be late, but I guess I forgot. Eleven turned to midnight and midnight turned to one and I was having a great time on the dance floor. All of a sudden, the music stopped and the DJ came on: "Will Michelle Cambria please come to the DJ booth?" I remember thinking, *That's funny. I wonder if we're related.* The music started up again for a few minutes and then it stopped yet again and I saw Dad, in his stiff white lieutenant's shirt, on one side of the dance floor, striding toward me. Everyone parted before him like he was Moses. He grabbed my arm and frog-marched me outside. Then he put me in the cop car, in the back, and we drove home. I didn't talk to him for weeks.

When you're an NYPD negotiator, failure can be a matter of life and death. But my dad rarely spoke to me about the times when things went wrong, when hostages died or jumpers jumped. I know he took every loss hard and carried it somewhere deep within him. But he never really showed us that. I wonder sometimes if he had someone to talk to. Yet I think he used all of it—all the love we had in our home and all his professional failures, too—to help him save lives. He once said that the key to being a good hostage negotiator is to love someone and to be loved, to know the bitter taste of loss and what despair actually feels like. Dad marshaled all of his life experience to save the lives of other people. As his daughter, I was both a part of that and privileged to benefit from his tremendous empathy.

Melissa Cambria is a fourth-grade teacher. She lives in Brooklyn, New York, with her husband and daughter.

Jack and Melissa (six years old) at the headquarters of Emergency Service
Squad 6 in Brooklyn, New York, 1992

My Father the Inventor

Ray Kurzweil

by Amy Kurzweil

Ray Kurzweil is an inventor, futurist, author, and philosopher, born in Queens, New York, in 1948. Among his many inventions are the CCD flatbed scanner, the omni-font optical character recognition system, a print-to-speech reading machine for the blind, and the first high-quality music synthesizer. He was one of the first scientists to predict the rise of artificial intelligence and has written eleven books on the subject. He is currently a director of engineering for Google. He and his wife, Sonya, have two children, Ethan and Amy.

M Y FATHER IS FAMOUS for being a big thinker, motivated by a desire to create a better future. He's also a provider, and is equally motivated to support his family. Though he now spends his days at the Googleplex, my father was inspired not by the tech gurus of Silicon Valley but by his artist parents and the legacy of his ancestors in Vienna (his great-grandmother started the first school in Europe that provided higher education for girls). From them he inherited a creative, entrepreneurial streak and a desire to do good.

His parents fled Vienna in 1938 and settled in Queens. His mother was an illustrator and a painter. His father was a classical pianist, conductor, and composer who made his living mostly through teaching; he passed away when my father was twenty-two. My grandfather struggled with the dueling responsibilities of honoring his passion and providing; a musician's life in America was much less lucrative than it had been in the city he was forced to flee. From an early age, my dad was driven to help the family get by, first in small ways (with a paper route, for example) and later, when his inventions began earning him prizes and awards, in more significant ones.

My father likes to brag that he knew he wanted to be an inventor—to change the world—at age five. But I suspect that this ambition transcended an individual desire for achievement and recognition. I believe he wanted to liberate his parents from financial hardship so they could pursue their passions, as they encouraged him to pursue his.

At fifteen, he wrote his first computer program: pattern recognition software that analyzed and imitated the works of classical composers, a harbinger of the Kurzweil synthesizer he'd invent in the 1980s. He graduated from MIT in 1970 with degrees in Computer Science and Creative Writing. In 1974, he started Kurzweil Computer Products, the company responsible for the Kurzweil Reading Machine, which helps the blind and those with reading impairments.

He sold KCP in 1980. My mother talks about this sale as a pivotal moment in our nuclear family history, one that finally gave us some financial stability.

In addition to being an innovative scientific thinker, my father has been a writer for as long as I've known him. When his first book, *The Age of Intelligent Machines*, came out in 1990, I was four. It was a giant book, literally. The cover was blue and purple and green and printed with futuristic 3-D spheres. I knew not everyone wrote a book, and I was proud my father had. I remember paging through it in bed when I was maybe ten. I couldn't understand the content. All I remember is the book's heft.

The Age of Spiritual Machines came out when I was thirteen, old enough to comprehend some of it. This book catered to less technologically savvy readers; at the end of each chapter was a dialogue with a fictional character named Molly, and the reports from her voyages into the future read like stories. These fictional interludes really helped me see the future world my father imagined. I don't remember if his vision surprised me. In my memory, his ideas are like his smell: they've just always been around.

My father deeply believes in his vision of the Singularity—that we'll soon spend more and more time in an increasingly immersive virtual reality, that AI will transform human life beyond our current imagination. He thinks technology and intelligence can solve any human problem. But while in his books and lectures he espouses these beliefs eloquently and passionately, he doesn't evangelize in private. He accepts other worldviews. Although ethnically Jewish, he grew up attending a Unitarian church. That faith's credo is "Many paths to the truth." I don't think my father feels that religious observance is incompatible with his techno-optimism, and he accedes to my mother's desire to participate in Jewish rituals. I think he sees many religious ideas as describing something like the Singularity, just with different words.

Publicly, my father is sometimes cast as an extremist: "Ray versus the Luddites." He's confident and can be stubborn, but he's also a good listener. Privately, if you tell him something he hasn't heard

Ray with Amy (thirteen years old) at her bat mitzvah in
Boston, 1999

before, he'll say, "That's interesting," and later incorporate the idea into his thinking. When he started at Google, he was honored to join an organization with such smart people who share his interests. Work has always been the most meaningful way for my father to connect with other people, including me.

The first time I worked with my dad in a professional capacity was in 2000, when he gave a TED Talk demonstrating the potential of virtual reality. Using motion capture technology, he transformed himself into a rock star named "Ramona." He'd move, and the avatar would move with him. The ludicrous transformation was meant to showcase a vision of a future in which you can be what you want to be. He needed backup and asked me to participate, since I, then fourteen years old, was a dancer and loved to perform. I was transformed in virtual reality into three big middle-aged men modeled on the organizer of the conference. (It was supposed to be funny.) The experience gave me a taste of the intensity of my father's world: weeks of hours-long rehearsals in a heavy suit, a trip from Boston to California, a packed audience, a film crew following us the whole time. It was both exhausting and exciting.

My father is an idealist. He has modeled a professional life of passion, and he's steered me away from compromising mine. He's worked tirelessly so he can think and create on his own terms and with the people he's loyal to. When I decided that I wanted to be a writer and an illustrator, to pick up the mantle of my grandparents and all the struggles the artistic life entails, I felt that the tenacity required for this path was in my blood. I'm grateful for a life in which I, like the virtual beings of my father's future, can be what I want to be.

Amy Kurzweil is a *New Yorker* cartoonist and the author of *Flying Couch: A Graphic Memoir.* She is working on her second graphic memoir, about her father and grandfather. She lives in Brooklyn, New York.

My Father the King of Cool

Miles Davis

by Erin Davis

Born in Alton, Illinois, in 1926, trumpeter and composer Miles Davis is widely considered the most influential jazz musician of the twentieth century. Davis's mercurial brilliance was reflected in his creative output, which was as prodigious as it was varied, ranging from his jazz masterpiece Kind of Blue *to the experimental* Bitches Brew. *He had four children, Gregory, Miles IV, Erin, and Cheryl. He died in 1991, at age sixty-five.*

Erin (age fourteen) and Miles on tour in Europe, 1985

P EOPLE THINK OF MY DAD as the prince of darkness (the name of his 1967 album), a moody performer who turned his back on the audience out of disregard for them. That wasn't him at all. But this wasn't something even I truly realized until I stood onstage with him as part of his legendary band: Dad wasn't turning away from the audience; he was turning *toward* the band. It wasn't a sign of disrespect for those there to hear him; it was a sign of respect for those there to play. And I was lucky enough to be there to play.

My parents separated before I was born, and for most of the school year, my father was out on tour. When I did see him, it tended to be at his studio. I knew he was a famous musician but didn't quite understand *how* famous. As a kid, I was always telling him I wanted to be a musician. Finally, when I was fourteen, he asked if I wanted to go on the road with him in the summer. Of course I said yes.

I learned a lot, not only about music but about my father, during those summer tours. As I stood in the wings, I saw that playing the music live was the most important thing to my dad. He had all these legendary musicians onstage. As the tour progressed, the songs would morph into different configurations, find different grooves, and get better. To accomplish that, he had to have a lot of contact with the musicians. He taught me that you can't just go out in front and smile at the crowd. You have to turn around. You have to make eye contact with everybody in the band and make sure they are watching you.

Those summer tours were the first and longest sustained amount of time I spent with my father. What I discovered about him was how he could break down what was going on in any musical performance or composition—and find something to take away from it. I remember once watching the old *Headbangers Ball* on MTV, and when Slayer came on, I thought, *Oh my God, Dad's going to hate this.* He watched for a bit and then said, "Huh. That drummer is really laying it down, isn't he?" Then he just walked away.

After a few summers of watching—me watching him and him watching me—he finally asked me onstage for a tour in 1990. He was giving me a chance, and I was terrified of blowing it. I played electronic percussion, which was a genre my dad kind of invented. Instead of having traditional percussionists, he would sample them and the percussionist would play those samples through an Octapad, a sort of triggering device. I didn't even get any rehearsals. I watched the guy who did it before me for a couple of shows, then I was just on it, in the seat. It was *my* gig. It was nerve-racking for me, but at the same time, it felt wonderful to have my father turn toward me, to listen to me and to play with me as an equal.

Erin Davis, along with his sister and cousin, is an executor of the Miles Davis estate. He lives in Santa Monica, California, with his two daughters.

My Father the Mentalist
Uri Geller

by Daniel Geller

For the last forty years, Uri Geller has straddled the line between magic and mysticism. In the 1970s, he rose to fame for his seeming ability to bend metal spoons using paranormal powers. Since then he has worked as a psychic, entertainer, television personality, and mineral dowser. Born in Tel Aviv, Israel, in 1946, Geller lived in Cyprus, the United States, and the United Kingdom before returning to Israel in 2015. He and his wife, Hannah, have two children, Daniel and Natalie.

Daniel (age four), Natalie (age three), and Uri, 1985

THOUGH I WAS BORN IN NEW YORK, I spent my childhood in Sonning-on-Thames, a small village forty miles west of London, in a big riverside property with my father, mother, younger sister, uncle Shipi (who was my father's manager), and grandmother, whom my father looked after. My father wasn't a disciplinarian, but he was strict when he had to be. He was very big on manners and insistent about etiquette, which was especially important since so many famous visitors—including Mohamed Al-Fayed, Michael Jackson, and various members of Parliament—often came to our house. He was also adamant that my sister and I be aware of how privileged we were. His childhood in Israel and later Cyprus was nowhere near as charmed as ours. We traveled the world with my dad, often staying in immense luxury, but he often took the opportunity to walk us through the slums so we never lost perspective.

Of course, growing up as the son of the world's most well-known mentalist had its own peculiarities. The paranormal world was very much a part of my childhood. Soon after we moved to England, when I was five or six, a thumb-size crystal fell out of a glass cabinet in the living room. My father and I were standing in the kitchen when we heard the noise. We rushed to see what had crashed. There was the crystal on the floor, yet the glass doors of the cabinet remained closed. The crystal must have teleported.

The next incident that sticks out happened a few years later. My father had received a request for a personal consultation. He did this sometimes, visiting the homes of both the famous and the non-famous. Often he'd bring me along. "Come on, Daniel," he'd say. "It's going to be fun." This time his client was an English actor named Sarah Miles who was convinced that her home was haunted. We hopped into Dad's Cadillac and headed over. Sarah greeted us at the door, and we began climbing these creaky stairs. We walked over to a windowsill in a sitting room. She began to tell us the significance of a jewelry box in the room, which I have since forgotten. My dad said, "Let's see if we can call up the ghost." He began to talk to the ghost, asking it to give us a sign if it could hear us, and the jewelry box slowly began to ascend into the air. Sarah and I watched wide-eyed. Dad didn't seem as surprised. There was no rational explanation for what had happened.

Both the teleportation and the poltergeist were the kinds of paranormal things that surrounded my father and that I witnessed. Dad took me along often to visit random strangers who claimed to be possessed by demons or other supernatural beings, too. I was never scared by them. Rather, I enjoyed the adventures.

In some ways, Dad's fame and the reason for it were a curse. As I said, I went to school in a small village where everyone knew who my father was. (It was impossible not to know—one day he had driven my sister and me to school in his Cadillac, which he had turned into a sculpture made of bent spoons.) I endured no small amount of abuse, both physical and verbal, much of which centered around my father. They called him a freak and me the son of a freak. But in countless ways, my father's gift has been a blessing. Once, I lost a library book and Dad used his energy to locate it. (It had fallen behind the cupboard.) Later, while I was at university, he'd send me positive energy, which I felt as I was sitting at the exam desk. Once, it even saved my life. It was the night of my dad's birthday, sometime in the late 1980s. My sister and I were playing in the marble foyer of our house, a big area with a massive crystal that my dad had acquired and installed on a pedestal. Natalie and I were sliding down the banister that ran from the second to the first floor. As I was sliding, I fell down onto the marble floor below from rather high up. There was a thud, and I began to bleed profusely. I could have been badly hurt or even died, but as it turned out, the only injuries I sustained were cuts on my chin and lip, from when my knees hit my chin.

The next morning, my father descended the stairs and came upon a ray of light being refracted through the crystal, sending rainbows through the room. This was December, and no sun shone in the sky. Something—or rather someone—must have been producing that ray.

My father surmised that it was the energy of the crystal. He said that this energy had saved my life. I didn't argue. I was, in fact, alive and relatively unhurt. Plus, I had no reason to disbelieve my father.

But, of course, the debate as to whether my father is truly a mentalist or a magician cannot simply be banished from our doors by the loyalty and love occasioned by familial bonds. I distinctly remember as a child being curious about whether what he does is a power or a talent. My father never told my sister and me—the topic was taboo—and after thirty-seven years, I have still never asked. Years ago, I told him, "Please never tell me the truth." No good would come of either posing or answering the question. I know what I saw. And I know that my father is a wonderful parent who gave me both a super and a normal childhood.

_____

Daniel Geller is a lawyer living in London, England.

My Father the Miracle Worker Herb Brooks

by Daniel Brooks

Herb Brooks was a professional hockey coach, born in Saint Paul, Minnesota, in 1980, the United States men's national hockey team, under Brooks's leadership, shocked the world by defeating the four-time defending gold medalist Soviet national hockey team in the semifinals of the Olympic Games at Lake Placid, New York. Dubbed the "Miracle on Ice," the game became a defining moment in the history of American sports. After the Olympics, Brooks continued coaching, notably with the New York Rangers. He and his wife, Patti, had two children, Daniel and Kelly. He died in 2003 at age sixty-six.

M Y FAVORITE TIMES WITH MY DAD always revolved around hockey. My fondest memories from when I was a kid are of when he would bring me on the road with him, all across the country, to watch high school recruits play. It was great getting to be there and spend those hours with my dad. And when he coached the New York Rangers when I was a teen, I would go with him to the team's home games at Madison Square Garden. Since we lived in Greenwich, Connecticut, at the time, we would have the car ride together before and after each game. We would talk about hockey, life, or whatever else came up. Those were the best times.

But in truth, my father was gone a lot. Being a coach meant he was on the road constantly, and often he couldn't take me with him. He worked tirelessly and put in long hours. In 1972, he was hired to turn around Minnesota's hockey program, so from that point on, whether it was recruiting players or studying tape, he always had something going on.

To be clear, he wasn't an absentee father. It was just the nature of the job—his profession demanded an extraordinary level of dedication, and from a young age, I understood that. Unlike a lot of kids with busy parents, I was lucky because it was always clear to me what my father was doing. And getting to cheer him on, whether watching from the stands or on TV when he was away, was huge for me. I was so proud of him.

My dad's defining moment came in 1980, when I was twelve years old. It was the semifinal hockey game of the Lake Placid Olympics: the United States versus the Soviet Union. I was there, sitting in the stands, with the rest of the world behind me. It really was like being in a movie, as this legendary game played out before our eyes. Here was our Cold War foe, whose athletes had been groomed nearly from birth, up against our scrappy all-amateur US team. It was more than a sporting event. It was a contest between cultures. We all knew immediately we were witnessing something important. It was one of the biggest moments—if not *the* biggest moment—in US sports history. It was the "Miracle on Ice." People still remember where they were during the game. And my dad wasn't simply a minor footnote in the story: he was the coach.

Dad knew how significant the game was as soon as it happened, and he predicted that its magnitude would only grow with time. He was right. When the movie *Miracle* came out in 2004, it reminded people of this incredible story and also introduced younger people to it for the first time. Even today, the Miracle on Ice stirs up emotion in people all around the country.

Before I headed off to the University of Denver to play hockey, my dad gave me some advice from the perspective of a coach: "Be the first one on the ice and the last one to leave, and keep your mouth shut." He was big on peace of mind and always insisted that no trophy or amount of money could ever be as rewarding as knowing that I'd done my best.

My dad was on the road too much to get involved with my amateur hockey career, but it was always special when he got to see me play. In my junior and senior years of college, he finally had some downtime because he was between coaching jobs. I loved that he was able to watch me play at an elite level—it was special for both of us. He came to every game.

Daniel Brooks is a financial adviser in Minneapolis, Minnesota, where he lives with his wife and their two daughters. He also sits on the board of the Herb Brooks Foundation.

Kelly, Patti, Daniel, and Herb at their home in Saint Paul, Minnesota, circa 1980

My Father the Murderer

George Hodel

by Steve Hodel

Born in Los Angeles, California, in 1907, George Hodel was chief of social hygiene for the Los Angeles County Department of Health from 1939 to 1945. He had eleven children. After his death at age ninety-one in 1999, he became a prime suspect in the infamous murder of Elizabeth Short in Los Angeles in 1947, commonly known as the Black Dahlia murder.

L ATE SPRING 1949, Los Angeles, a perfect day. The sun broke through the clouds as our family climbed into the squeaky-clean Willys MB military jeep Dad had purchased the year before. Mother got into the passenger seat while my two brothers and I—Mike, nine; me, seven; and Kelvin, six—scrambled into the back. Dad cranked up the engine, and we were off, headed to Pismo Beach for a day of swimming in the ocean and digging for clams near the shore.

The drive from Hollywood, where we lived and where Dad had once served as the head of the Los Angeles County Department of Health, was about four hours, so we arrived near the pier at noon. Dad put the jeep in low gear, and down onto the sandy beach we went, headed south to the clam beds. After driving about two miles, we came to a small stream. Dad had timed it perfectly. We arrived at low tide and easily crossed the stream.

Dad continued south, passing the large posted sign that read, "Baby Clam Fields. No Digging. Fifty-Dollar Fine Per Clam."

"All right, boys, everyone out. Let's find out where they're hiding."

I paused for a moment to register how easily he'd disregarded the posted rules. Clam shovels and pails in hand, we three boys spread out, each of us staking out our own territory in the wet sand.

Dad, standing next to the jeep, lit a large cigar and yelled out, "A dollar goes to the boy who finds the most clams." Within a half hour, each of our buckets was filled. We had collected maybe seventy-five clams all told. Dad placed the buckets behind the rear seat, covering them with a blanket, and broke out the inflatable rubber raft, which we boys took turns blowing up.

We enjoyed another two hours of fun in the sun, swimming and riding the waves to shore in our bright yellow "landing craft." High tide was approaching. We dried off, changed out of our wet swim trunks, dressed, and started back to the pier. As we approached what earlier had been a small stream, we saw what now was more like a raging river.

My father confidently edged the jeep into the water. We got almost all the way across before the engine coughed, sputtered, and stopped about ten feet from dry sand. We were stuck. In the distance, we could see a truck moving toward us. It stopped on the hard sand and two uniformed men, fish and game wardens, got out.

Dad took out his wallet, flashed a silver badge, and yelled to them, "I am Dr. Hodel, head of the LA County health department. We seem to be stuck. Can you give us a tow?"

The older of the two responded, "Sure, Doc. Hang on. We'll get you out."

Dad turned to Mother and the three of us and said, "Don't say a word. Not a word." Our haul of baby clams underneath the towel could have resulted in $3,750 worth of fines. In today's dollars, that's nearly $40,000. The younger man waded out into the water to the front of the jeep and attached a heavy chain, and we were pulled out in a flash.

Dad smiled and shook their hands. "Took the boys swimming and lost track of time. The tide came in faster than I expected. Here's my card. If you get down to LA, lunch is on me."

We stopped halfway home, in Santa Barbara. Dad pulled the jeep to the rear of a fancy seaside restaurant, gave us a stern "Wait here," and strolled to the front of the restaurant. Five minutes passed, and out he came with a man in a white apron and tall chef's hat. He took him to the rear of the jeep and removed the blanket, and the man said, "You've got yourself a deal."

A few minutes later, we were seated at a large table with a great ocean view. Dinner was served: a large Caesar salad followed by linguini with a rich white clam sauce.

Dad had brokered a "trade." The chef agreed to cook and serve us some of our baby clams—a free dinner—and the restaurant got to keep the rest of the haul.

Fifty years later, when my father died, I held on to this day as if it were encased in amber. Here was a man so cool under pressure

George (back left) with his sons (clockwise from back right) Duncan (fifteen years old), Mike (four years old), Kelvin (one year old), and Steve (two years old), 1943

and debonair he could get away with anything. But I had no idea how much he had actually gotten away with. In his lifetime, Dad was well-acquainted with scandal. In 1949, the same year we had gone clamming at Pismo Beach, he was arrested for molesting my older half sister, Tamar. Shortly after the trial—during which he was acquitted despite there having been three witnesses to his acts—he fled the country. He wouldn't return until 1990.

After he died, Tamar started talking to me about our father. During one of our conversations, she told me he had been a suspect in the Black Dahlia murder, the 1947 death of twenty-two-year-old Elizabeth Short. It was Los Angeles's most infamous unsolved case. After a twenty-four-year career as an LAPD detective, seventeen years of which were spent in the homicide division, I was familiar with the case. But I had never heard my dad's name associated with it. My immediate response was, "Tamar, what the hell are you talking about? Where is this coming from?"

"Well, the detectives that took me to court told me they suspected him of killing the Black Dahlia back then," she replied. "I don't think he did it, but that's what they said."

I was shocked. I loved my father. He was never warm or fuzzy, but he was a truly remarkable man who had lived an amazing life.

I was confident I could quickly clear my father of any suspicion. I knew I could exonerate him. And so I started to do the detective work I had spent my career undertaking. My initial investigation, much to my surprise, revealed that two years prior to the Black Dahlia murder, in May 1945, my father had been investigated by LAPD detectives for the suspected forced overdose (drugging by pills) of his twenty-seven-year-old personal secretary and lover, Ruth Spaulding. However, the evidence was insufficient to formally charge him, and when my father left to work as a doctor in China, authorities were forced to shut down the investigation and rule the suspicious death a suicide. I had never known.

A year and a half after I began looking into the Black Dahlia case, after interviewing dozens of witnesses, reviewing thousands of pages of investigative research, and separating the wheat (facts) from the chaff (fiction), I had my answer. I assembled the results of my investigations and presented them in secret to an active LA head deputy district attorney. He reviewed the materials and provided me with his legal opinion: "The Black Dahlia is solved and the crime was committed by Dr. George Hill Hodel." However, since my father had died, there was no formal investigation.

Two decades have passed since I established my father's guilt. I wrote a book about it and have, since then, discovered twenty-four other likely victims of my father's reign of terror. During those two decades, I have been through every conceivable emotion. Disbelief gave way to depression, followed by anger, hatred, and rage. Now those emotions have all melded together into sadness.

I still love my father. After all, he created me, gave me life and breath. His blood is flowing through my veins at this very moment. How can I not love him? But he was, without a doubt, a monster.

I love my father. I hate my father. He was a true-life Jekyll and Hyde. I look back on those memories of Pismo Beach, at the arrogance and ease with which my father disregarded the rules, and wonder if that was perhaps a sign of his darker self. Charming. Manipulative. Callous. Cruel. Daring. Charismatic. I shudder to think how else my father deployed those traits when he wasn't with us. But I can't lie, either. I hold those early childhood memories dear, like baby clams, best left undisturbed and protected, and wrong to pry open.

Steve Hodel is a retired LAPD homicide detective and the author of five books about his father's crimes, including, most recently, *Black Dahlia Avenger III: Murder as a Fine Art*. He lives in Los Angeles, California.

My Father the Novelist Kurt Vonnegut

by Mark Vonnegut

Widely considered one of America's greatest novelists, Kurt Vonnegut was born in Indianapolis, Indiana, in 1922. During World War II, Vonnegut served in the army and was captured soon after deployment in the Battle of the Bulge. His wartime experiences inspired or influenced many of his best-known works, including Player Piano, Mother Night, Cat's Cradle, *and* Slaughterhouse-Five. *From 1945 to 1971, he was married to Jane Marie Cox, and they had three biological children and four adopted children. In 1979, he married Jill Krementz, with whom he had one adopted daughter. He died in 2007 at age eighty-four.*

Had my father not been a writer, he would have been another broken vet. After World War II, he suffered from severe post-traumatic stress disorder. He used to tell me stories of being captured by Germans in the Battle of the Bulge and being beaten almost to death. He was only in his twenties when he witnessed the fire bombings of Dresden from the slaughterhouse where he and the other prisoners were kept. Being forced to clean the burnt bodies from a civilian bomb shelter was the defining experience of his life. He dealt with that pain by becoming a writer. But whereas so many of my father's readers identified with the horrors of Dresden through the eyes of Billy Pilgrim, the time traveling protagonist of *Slaughterhouse-Five*, I knew that it was his own inner demons he was expelling onto the page.

I'm deeply grateful that he found his way, but, of course, a writer's life is not without its challenges. My father had grown up fairly wealthy in Indianapolis. Before the Great Depression, his family had a cook and a servant. But the Depression wiped that all out, and when he came back from the war, he really struggled to make a living.

I grew up relatively poor, surrounded by a lot of arguments about money. My father worked hard writing and rewriting short stories, trying to get them published. He shuffled around the house mumbling. In fact, we all knew that the more he mumbled, the less he was writing and the better it was to steer clear of him. In the 1950s, the market for the type of short fiction my dad wrote was dying, so he was forced to do a lot of other things to make ends meet. He tried to sell cars for a while, but he was terrible at it. He taught English at Cape Cod Community College and at the Hopefield School, a school for troubled kids in Massachusetts. He took a job in advertising, and even had a one-day stint working as a staff writer for *Sports Illustrated*. (They wanted him to write a story about a racehorse who broke away and jumped over a fence. He sat at his desk all morning, trying to figure out how to write the story. Finally, he typed out, "The horse jumped over the fucking fence," and quit.)

We were a big family. My two younger sisters were born in 1949 and 1954, and in 1958, my parents adopted my aunt's four orphaned children after she died of cancer and her husband died a day later when his train plunged off a bridge into the water below. We lived in a sprawling house in Cape Cod. Parts of it were two hundred years old. There was a big barn and a beautiful pond, but the property was definitely run-down. I knew that my father was stressed out about money. You could sense it in the atmosphere. I think he felt resentful that having so many family obligations ate into his creative time. I know he struggled with the fact that he wasn't as widely hailed as Hemingway or Fitzgerald. That wasn't just ego but also about his ability to keep us all fed and housed. As his oldest son, I carried some of that worry, too. Once, he borrowed a hundred dollars from me from my paper route. I was happy to give it to him.

Around this time, in an effort to make some money, he developed a board game called General Headquarters. It was a game of strategy played on a chessboard. You had eight divisions of infantry, three artillery, one paratrooper, two armored artillery, and a heavy artillery. You had to focus two of your pieces on one of the opposition's to kill it. My father—who was a tremendous draftsman (having inherited the skill from his father, an architect)—went through several rounds of designs before he was satisfied. Then he headed out to the barn to cut the game pieces out of wood on an old band saw and painstakingly painted them. At last, we were ready to play.

I often played board games with my father. But he never took it easy on me, nor I on him. My father had a temper, and he didn't handle losing very well. Eventually my siblings got so tired of searching for pieces lost after he flung the board across the room, they asked me to not win so often. But I wasn't inclined to throw a game and didn't. Nevertheless, I became his guinea pig for General Headquarters. It was a really, really good game. And I loved playing it with him, working out the kinks. I felt like I was contributing to the

Kurt with Mark (four months old) in Schenectady,
New York, 1947

family work. (I had the same delightful feeling when, as a teenager proofreading *The Sirens of Titan*, I found a quotation mark missing.)

My dad's idea was that the game would help World War II veterans like himself who wanted to show off their skills at strategy in a nonviolent way. It was a pacifist war game. Unfortunately, like so many of my father's endeavors, this one failed, too. He tried to sell it to game companies like Milton Bradley and Saalfield Game Company. Milton Bradley never expressed interest in it. He was turned down by Saalfield, too; they thought it was too complicated. So he and I are the only two who have ever played the game. I still have the pieces, wrapped in a cloth in a drawer in my home—little totems of my father's genius, born of necessity and trauma.

Mark Vonnegut is a pediatrician in Quincy, Massachusetts. He is the author of the memoirs *The Eden Express: A Memoir of Insanity* and *Just Like Someone Without Mental Illness Only More So.*

My Father the Organizer

Cesar Chavez

by Paul F. Chavez

Cesar Estrada Chavez, born in 1927 outside Yuma, Arizona, was a farm labor organizer and civil rights leader who began the National Farm Workers Association (later called the United Farm Workers union) in 1962. He led the famous Delano grape strike, which lasted five years and ended with the UFW getting their first union contract with growers in the area. Beyond organizing strikes and marches, Chavez focused on pushing legislation that protected farmworkers. He and his wife, Helen Fabela, raised eight children, Elizabeth, Anna, Linda, Sylvia, Paul, Fernando, Eloise, and Anthony. Chavez died in 1993 at age sixty-six and is buried at the National Chavez Center in Kern County, California.

Paul and Cesar discussing handball strategy in California, 1970s

I REMEMBER ONCE, when I was about ten years old, writing my name on the ceiling above my dad's bed. I assume it was my way of saying, "Hey, Dad, don't forget about us." Unlike other fathers, my dad didn't take me to Little League games. I don't remember doing a lot of things my friends did with their fathers, because my dad was on the road, organizing and building the farmworker movement. One of the many sacrifices he made was not spending time with his children.

After high school, in part to find a way to connect with my dad, I decided to work full-time with the United Farm Workers union. I wanted to be an organizer, but my father promptly put me to work at the UFW's print shop, running the presses—something I knew nothing about and had no interest in. But I became a pretty good printer, and eventually I came to enjoy it.

After I spent a few years at the print shop, my dad asked me to work as an assistant in his office. I resisted. By this time, I had grown to love the print shop. I thought I'd been born with ink in my veins. Besides, I had never worked in an office. I finally joined his staff, did well, and became interested in how plans and budgets were made, how to identify issues and allocate resources to solve problems— tools I still use today.

By then, the union had achieved much success in organizing workers. It needed negotiators to bargain union contracts. Some union leaders wanted to hire experienced outside negotiators. My father was convinced that the sons and daughters of farmworkers could learn those skills. But they would need training and opportunities to make mistakes while learning.

This was one of the important *consejos*, or life lessons, I learned from my father, and which still offers me direction: have faith in people. At the heart of our movement is the unfailing faith my dad had in the poorest and least educated—a belief that they could challenge one of California's mightiest industries and prevail. My dad understood that individual lives and successive generations would be forever changed and people uplifted if they were given the chance to negotiate their own union contracts. He asked me to be a part of it. I was content to be an administrative assistant. But he insisted, and I joined the first class of fifteen students training to become negotiators at a school he established at our headquarters. It was a tough yearlong academic curriculum. We worked hard, made some mistakes, but gained confidence going up against seasoned grower negotiators, many of them lawyers.

After that experience, I thought my calling was as a negotiator. Then my father asked me to become the union's political director and lobbyist. That also took convincing. Though I had seen him up close as an organizer, I knew nothing about lobbying and very little of how to navigate the legislative process. I'd learn quickly. At the time, new, hostile administrations were taking over in Washington and Sacramento. The incoming California governor campaigned on dismantling the historic state farm labor law, which let workers organize, that my dad had worked hard to pass under Governor Jerry Brown.

After a couple of years, my father pushed me to leave the lobbying and political job to take over and expand what today is the Cesar Chavez Foundation, which helps workers and other poor people with the crippling dilemmas they face off the job site and in the community. I asked myself, *What do I know about affordable housing and educational radio?* But my dad was confident I could do the job.

Looking back, I realize that at every step of the way, I was unsure I could do the jobs my father thought I could. I lacked confidence, yet my father was persistent. He encouraged and pushed me at each turn. And I came to realize that he had more faith in me than I had in myself.

Today, the foundation takes part in Cesar Chavez commemorations across the nation. I meet men and women my father personally influenced—and they tell me their stories. There was the young teacher's aide whom my dad convinced to become a teacher. She went on to become an administrator, and today she is a district superintendent. There was the nurse who became a doctor at my dad's urging. And there was a paralegal, the son of striking farm-workers, who was challenged by my father to become a lawyer. He is now a superior court judge in Kern County, California.

My father gave people opportunities no one would have given him when he was a migrant kid with an eighth-grade education. Whenever he met young people, especially if they came from farm-worker or working-class families, my dad challenged them to believe in themselves and their capabilities. He helped hundreds fulfill dreams many didn't even know they had at the time.

The faith my father had in me, he had in an entire community as well. He trusted people to create their own future.

The second lesson I learned from my dad was perseverance.

In 1982, as the union's political director, I led a statewide cam-paign in California to confirm a nominee to the farm labor board and ensure enforcement of the farm labor law. My father and I joined hundreds of farmworkers watching the final vote in the gallery above the ornate Senate chamber at the state capitol in Sacramento. We were one vote short.

I was devastated. Around 10:00 p.m., after my dad offered encouraging words to the workers, he said to me, "Let's drive home." It was about five hours from Sacramento to our headquarters in Keene, near Bakersfield.

After about an hour on the road, my father asked how I was doing. I told him I felt I had let him, the farmworkers, and the movement down. I felt terrible.

"Did you do everything you could do?" my dad asked.

"Yes," I answered.

"Did you leave any stone unturned?"

"No, I did everything I knew how to do."

"Did you work as hard as you could?"

"Yes, I did."

"Remember," my father said, "our work isn't like a baseball game, where after nine innings, whoever has the most runs wins and the other team loses.

"It's not a political race, where each candidate runs a campaign and on Election Day whoever gets the most votes wins and everyone else loses.

"In our work, La Causa, the fight for justice, you only lose when you stop fighting—you only lose when you quit."

Then he added, "Let's go home and get some rest, because tomorrow we have a lot of work to do."

People forget that Cesar Chavez had more defeats than victories. Yet each time he was knocked to the ground, he'd pick himself up, dust himself off, and return to the nonviolent fight. The lesson was clear: Victory is ours when we refuse to give up.

Paul F. Chavez is the president and chairman of the Cesar Chavez Foundation. He lives in Keene, California, and is the father of four children.

My Father the Physicist

Michio Kaku

by Michelle Kaku

Michio Kaku, born in San Jose, California, in 1947, is a theoretical physicist and professor at the City College of New York and CUNY Graduate Center. He is the father of the string field theory, a quantum leap toward a grand unified theory of everything. As a bestselling author, on-air personality, and regular guest on talk shows and science programs, Kaku has also become one of the country's most well-known disseminators of scientific information to a general audience. He and his wife, Shizue, have two daughters, Alyson and Michelle.

Michio helping Michelle (eleven years old) prepare to perform at her uncle's wedding, 1995

WHENEVER I THINK OF MY FATHER, the first image that comes to my mind is him twirling a lock of his long, wavy hair with his left hand and drawing equations in the air with his right, all the while looking off into space. "I get paid to think," he used to tell me. "It's the best job in the world." He was constantly ruminating. When I was in high school, my father would look over my shoulder while I studied at our dining room table for the New York State Regents Exams, the mandatory statewide standardized tests, and become visibly frustrated. "Why are you memorizing these lists of rocks?" he'd ask, gesturing to my study guide for the Earth Sciences section of the test. "When are you going to use this information? No wonder our youth are not going into the sciences!"

To him, the fact that children weren't being inspired by their school curriculum to pursue careers in the sciences was a grievous mistake. This is why he took it upon himself to show my sister, Alyson, and me just how exciting and practical these fields could be. He used to leave out big, evocative science books, like Isaac Asimov's *Biographical Encyclopedia of Science and Technology*, filled with pictures and ideas far more fantastic than the sort of stuff we learned in school. And he'd bring home DIY science kits—I was in awe when we managed to illuminate a lightbulb with little more than some copper wire and a magnet.

As my sister and I got older, he never stopped opening our eyes to the wonders of science. The experiments simply grew more complex. In high school, my father helped me build a Wilson cloud chamber, a particle detector that tracks the path of ionized radiation. We trekked all over New York City, heading to the Lower East Side for dry ice and to Chinatown to find craftsmen willing to make us a specialized plastic cylinder we could use for our cloud chamber. Once we'd obtained radioactive isotope samples through the mail, we put it all together and watched as the ionized particles left tiny curving trails in the piece of velvet cloth we'd placed inside the chamber, capturing their movements with a fancy new digital camera we'd purchased for the experiment.

Looking back, I think explaining the complicated ideas behind these projects to us kids helped him figure out how to communicate about science to the masses. The way he describes scientific topics on television and radio programs now is the same way he used to explain them to us in private.

Dad also encouraged us to be creative. He fostered my sister's love of painting and making pottery. He sat with me for hours while I practiced the violin, listening to me play the same passages over and over again without ever seeming to mind. And he took us ice-skating every week, eventually becoming an avid skater himself. He and our mom urged us to follow our dreams, whatever they might be, just as long as we pursued them to the best of our ability. He'd say to us, "If you find that your passion is garbage collecting, that's fine, but then you better be the best garbage collector ever."

When my sister fell in love with cooking and baking, my parents purchased new cooking utensils for the kitchen, helped her organize special cooking nights at the apartment, and encouraged her to seek out internships at prestigious restaurants. Now Alyson is a successful pastry chef.

For a while, I thought I wanted to go into theoretical physics like my father. But in college, I realized that I enjoyed interacting with and helping people, which didn't really fit with the frequently sequestered lifestyle of a physicist. So I chose a different path in the sciences and went to medical school, where I studied neurology. Today, it's my job to motivate and educate the next generation. Thankfully, years of sitting with my father has given me a lifetime of practice in watching inspiration catch fire.

Michelle Kaku, **MD,** is the director of the neurology residency program and an assistant professor of neurology at Boston University School of Medicine. She and her husband live in Boston, Massachusetts.

My Father the Pitcher Nolan Ryan

by Reid Ryan

Nolan Ryan was born in 1947 in Refugio, Texas. A fastball pitcher with a deadly curve, Ryan played for a number of Major League Baseball teams but is most identified with the Houston Astros and the Texas Rangers. He holds the all-time record for no-hitters, at seven, and was named an All-Star player eight times. He married Ruth Holdorff in 1967, and they have three children, Reid, Reese, and Wendy.

Reid and Nolan posing before a Houston Astros game
in the 1980s

M Y DAD GREW UP WANTING TO BE A RANCHER, not a Ranger. He bought a calf before he was ten, rented a small plot of land for it to live on, and bottle-fed it. You could do things like that in Refugio, Texas, in the 1950s. It was an idyllic town with big oak trees and an incredible Little League field, where my father learned to throw.

My dad went pro with the Mets in 1966 (and won the World Series with them in 1969), then got traded to the California Angels just after I was born in 1971, but Alvin, Texas, was always home—at least in the off-season. He wanted to be near the horses and cows and bird dogs. In the 1970s, West Coast games weren't televised in Texas, and there was no interleague play to bring the Angels closer to home. So, for a while, my dad was just another guy in town. One off-season, he pumped gas. Another, he attended community college.

In 1980, the Houston Astros signed my father to the first million-dollar MLB contract, and we began living in Texas full-time. My father's nickname up north had been Big Tex because he was sort of a hometown-boy cliché: He liked being outside and led a simple family life. He had started dating my mother when he was fifteen. When he moved home, he was still Big Tex, but as a local icon, not a curiosity.

In Alvin, we lived on one hundred acres outside of town in an old remodeled farmhouse. We had a backstop and an infield, and when I was in Little League—and even high school—my team would come over to practice. My dad would try to throw batting practice some-times, but he was bad at it. He was a 100-percent-effort guy. He couldn't throw slow. He'd hit you or bounce it. But when the kids on the team asked to see a Major League pitch, he'd show them what the real deal looked like. Maybe not the 108.5 mph fastball he threw in 1974, but something close.

Naturally, I wanted to be a pitcher. But my father was so advanced, it was hard for him to give me guidance—at least at first. I worked on mechanics with Astros pitching coach Tom House when I was getting started on the mound in my teens. My dad cut in only after I understood the basics. He taught me about the mental side of the game when I was considering playing college ball. He taught me how to be the 100-percent-effort guy.

Because he was big and threw hard, people didn't always understand that he made subtle adjustments and decisions to confuse batters. He prepped, and he had amazing mental discipline. My dad used to say, "Don't let the failure of your last pitch ruin the success of your next one." It was kind of a mantra. He always knew who swung at the first pitch and who couldn't hit a curve. He'd make undisciplined batters chase the ball out of the zone, and he'd stare down the batters he thought he could scare. He understood what he couldn't control and moved forward.

During the years we lived in Alvin, my dad played for some bad teams. In 1987, he went 8–16 and led the league in ERA. He was the most dominant pitcher in baseball, but his team didn't win because they didn't score. He would have had a remarkable record if he'd been back in New York, but he never complained—not in public and not in private. He just thought about the next pitch.

My dad came to watch me play when he could, though he was on the road a lot. It got harder as I got older. He was too famous to sit in the stands. By the time I was pitching for Texas Christian University, he couldn't come to a game without spending the whole thing signing autographs. So one time, he slipped into our dugout, just to watch the game in peace. We were playing the University of Texas, and their legendary coach Cliff Gustafson complained. It was against the rules for someone unaffiliated with the team to be in the dugout. We didn't have an assistant pitching coach at the time and my dad had just retired, so he signed up and wore the uniform. The pitcher with the most strikeouts in the history of Major League Baseball had become our assistant coach.

I remember a game we played against Texas A&M. They had these boisterous fans who were ragging us the whole time. One kid spent the entire game yelling at me and my dad. He said some pretty unsavory stuff. My dad didn't react. He had a tough exterior, but he was mostly a fun guy to be around—lots of horseplay and jokes. He kept it pretty light. Still, he was annoyed.

That night, we went out to dinner, and the kid who had been heckling us was there. My dad walked over to his table, put his hands on the kid's shoulders, and said, "You have fun at the game today?" The kid completely froze. My dad could have confronted him and made an ugly scene, but he's not like that. He congratulated him on the win while letting him know who was the bigger man. By the end of the meal, the kid was asking for his autograph.

In 1996, I got released from the New York–Penn League. I'd had a strong season in Class A, going .500 with a low ERA. But I hadn't crossed the picket line during the strike in 1994, which brought baseball and my career to a halt, and I'd gotten off to a slow start when games resumed. I went 0–10 between two leagues. When I found out about my release, I started blaming the strike and other people. I wasn't being honest and admitting that I wasn't very good. So my dad talked to me. "How many of the people you first played with got to play high school ball?" he asked. "How many got to play college ball? How many got to play professionally? You had an unbelievable career." He told me to keep trying to play if I wanted, but that he was going to be proud even if I decided to move on. So I took a different route. I got involved in the minors as an executive and an owner. In 1993, I became president of the Houston Astros.

Watching the Astros win the World Series in 2017 was as close as I ever got to the intensity of watching my father pitch. I had an emotional connection with the guys, and we were trying to achieve something together. But still, it wasn't the same as watching my dad out there, stalking around the mound, thinking about his next pitch, whipping his big body toward the batter.

It's different watching someone you love. It's different when it's your dad.

Reid Ryan is the president of the Houston Astros. He lives with his wife and their three children on a ranch in Houston, Texas.

My Father the Preacher Ted Haggard

by Marcus Haggard

Ted Haggard is a preacher, born in Yorktown, Indiana, in 1956. As the president of the National Association of Evangelicals, Haggard was an important voice in the rise of the evangelical movement in the 1980s. Besides founding and presiding as the pastor of the New Life Church in Colorado Springs, Colorado, Haggard frequently consulted with American political leaders. In 2006, however, Haggard's drug use and relationship with a male prostitute became public, causing him to leave his position at New Life. He has since founded a new church, the St. James Church. He and his wife, Gayle, have been married since 1978 and have five children, Christy, Marcus, Jonathan, Alex, and Elliott.

S OME OF MY EARLIEST MEMORIES are from New Life, the church my dad started. At that time, the small congregation met in our basement. There was a low-pile blue carpet, a little podium he would preach from, and folding chairs. My father performed baptisms in a local lake.

Surprisingly, my upbringing was not overly religious. I had faith. But my dad tried not to overburden the family with the ministry, so I didn't feel like it defined my life. That said, it was clear he wanted us children to participate with him in it if we were willing. In my dad's eyes, helping people was something we should do as a family. Having a father who was a preacher led to some interesting dynamics as a kid. For instance, my social sphere was made up of a wildly eclectic group of people ranging from respectable professionals to eccentric missionaries to the occasional town crazy, all connected by my father's church.

Somewhat atypical for a pastor, my dad was open to discussing my differing views on religion and politics. He wasn't very dogmatic. Both of my parents, in fact, allowed space for doubt. After a sermon, I'd sit with my dad, asking questions about what he had said and thinking of counterarguments. He would laugh, then we'd hash it out together. We'd debate original sin, the history and origins of the Bible, evolution and intelligent design. We talked about that last one a lot. Both my dad and I have an interest in science and nature. When he was a boy, the Apollo space program caught his interest, and he passed that interest on to me. He had a love of space and astronomy. The Colorado sky was so clear, we'd lay on the grass outside our house and look up at the stars or clouds. He'd point out cloud shapes or constellations, and we'd talk about what might be out there.

Though he grew busier as the church expanded, Dad tried to make time for his family. He loved to come to my soccer games. He's a very talkative guy, so he'd get to know everyone on the sidelines.

When I was in high school, he helped me operate a hay business. I would bring the hay from out of state and store it in our barn to sell to local farms. We owned horses when I was growing up, and every Saturday, he would join all five of us kids out in the barn, mucking stalls. He loved to work with us.

As teenagers, my friends and I would often head to the mountains to goof off. I remember once in high school, the night of a father-and-son campout organized by Dad's church, my friends and I went up and camped across the valley from the church group. We smoked and built a giant fire and were generally disruptive until around 4:00 a.m., when we finally passed out. When I woke up, my dad, my uncle, and five or six of the pastoral staff—along with their sons—were sitting among us by the fire. We were busted; cigarette butts and evidence of the night's carousing were strewn about. But the guys were all just friendly, refusing to mention the obvious signs of our deviancy, which made the experience all the more painful. Later that day, my dad pulled me aside and told me frankly: "The issue with making this type of decision is that, in the long run, it will hurt you. You should always be trustworthy, and decisions like this will cause people to lose trust in you."

When I was twenty-seven and recently married, Dad was at the center of a very public scandal. The destruction of trust in my father weighed heavily on my mind at the time and was, perhaps, one of the saddest parts of that event. I didn't actually experience that episode as a betrayal, or even really as a breach of trust. But I know that others felt that way. My father valued people placing their trust in him, so to feel that he had violated that trust was crushing to him.

When the allegations against my dad were made, my parents called all of us kids over to the house. We sat around the living room, and he told us that there was some truth to them. Soon thereafter, under a severance agreement with the New Life Church, my dad was required to move out of the state. He was distraught. So was I. It's hard for anyone to watch their dad lose his life's work. It was very hard for me. I was launching my career and had just started a family. I was building my world when my father's disintegrated.

Ted and Marcus (twenty years old) at the groundbreaking for New Life Church's new auditorium, 2004

He used to tell me when I was a kid that you're able to see the core of a person by watching how they respond in their darkest hour. As I had seen him do many times throughout my life, in the midst of all this chaos, he immersed himself in the Bible. He spent hours reading scripture and praying, morning and evening. He said that all he could do was keep trying to do the right thing, day by day, even if he didn't know where his efforts would lead. I don't think he knew it, but I was in the same mode: head down, just trying to do the right thing one day at a time until the dust settled.

The scandal had a silver lining, though. When I was growing up, struggling to get through college and then trying to find a job, my dad was a high-profile religious leader. He was frequently in the news and flying around the world meeting with all types of highly influential people. He tried to make time for me, but he was doing so much. His life felt distant from mine for years. Watching him struggle allowed me to see him in a very human way. I find I can relate more easily to him now. Plus, he's around much more. He and my mom live just forty-five minutes away from my family. Every Sunday, we can see him doing what he loves, teaching the Bible at St. James Church, a new church he leads in Colorado Springs. It's smaller than New Life, but he seems more joyful and more at peace than I ever remember him being. He frequently goes to the mountains to ride ATVs with friends. And he has much more time to hang out with my kids. They play games and gaze at the sky, just as I did with him as a child. He attends all their recitals and sports games.

There's a line from Romans that I think of when I look out my window and see my dad horsing around with my kids: "We know that all things work together for good for those who love God."

––––––––––––

Marcus Haggard is an attorney specializing in civil litigation, international investigations, and white-collar crime. He lives in Denver, Colorado, with his wife and their three children.

My Father the Scientist

Jonas Salk

by Peter L. Salk

Born in New York City in 1914, Jonas Salk was a virologist and research scientist who led the University of Pittsburgh team that developed the first successful polio vaccine in 1955. In 1960, he founded the Salk Institute for Biological Studies in La Jolla, California. From 1939 to 1968, he was married to Donna Salk, with whom he had three sons, Peter, Darrell, and Jonathan. In 1970, he married the French painter Françoise Gilot. Salk died at the age of eighty in 1995.

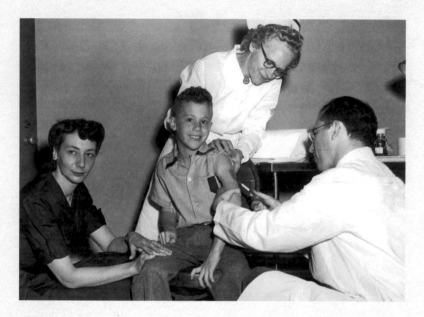

Peter receiving a polio shot from Jonas with the help of a nurse (as his mother, Donna, looks on), 1953

M Y FATHER was not a person with an off switch. He was extremely passionate and driven by his research. His dedication to his work kept him at the laboratory for long stretches of time. Because he and I were so rarely alone together when I was a boy, my memories of those times are precious to me. For instance, I was three years old when my younger brother Darrell was born. My father stayed home from work and took care of me while my mother was in the hospital. I remember that he made me scrambled eggs with ketchup, which I absolutely loved. I can still see us there in the kitchen, him at the stove, and taste the ketchup on those scrambled eggs.

Soon after Darrell was born, we moved from Ann Arbor, Michigan, to a house forty-five minutes outside of Pittsburgh. The home was in a fairly rural area, one of a small line of houses along Route 19, then a two-lane road. Both of my parents were city kids—my father grew up in the Bronx, and my mother grew up in Manhattan. But my father really wanted our family to experience a country environment, for which I am ever grateful. I grew up catching butterflies and playing in the fields and woods. Even when we moved into Pittsburgh proper in 1953, we continued to experience a country setting during summer vacations, when we'd stay in a rental cottage at Oberlin Beach on Lake Erie, a bit west of Cleveland. The only telephone during our first summers there was housed in a wooden box attached to a telephone pole at the side of the gravel road, and it was shared by the cottages in the small community. I remember my father walking out to the phone to speak with Lorraine, his secretary, or with the other scientists back at the lab. They were feverishly working on a vaccine to prevent polio, a disease that paralyzed and crippled primarily children, and which, at that time, was ravaging the country. In 1952, the worst year on record, there were around 58,000 cases of polio that resulted in more than 3,000 deaths.

I knew from my early years that my father was a physician and a scientist, and I could see the respect others had for him. Always wrapped up in his work, he would frequently come home from the lab at night with a small piece of paper containing reminders tucked under his tie clip. My brothers and I occasionally found ourselves in the unwelcome position of being on the receiving end of his experimental work. Two years before the vaccine against polio was released, he gave us our first injections in the kitchen. He brought home glass syringes and reusable needles, and boiled them on our stove to sterilize them. My mother then lined us up to get our shots. I remember once hiding behind the large wastebasket next to the refrigerator in an attempt to avoid being captured and put through the ordeal. Darrell once hid under his bed and had to be dragged out. I'm sure my parents explained to us what we were being injected with and why, but whatever explanation they gave didn't provide much comfort. The worst moments were when my father drew blood from our arms to test how the vaccine was working. I was still quite little then, and my veins were small and hard to find; I was greatly relieved when the vein in my arm finally grew large and easy to access when necessary.

When the work on the polio vaccine came to the public's attention, and particularly when the success of the national field trial of the safety and effectiveness of the vaccine was announced in April 1955, my father became quite well-known. He appeared on the cover of *Time* magazine and was hailed as a hero. Though he had mixed feelings about the degree of recognition he received, he realized the importance of his role as a communicator with the public and embraced it. He also saw the value of his success with the polio vaccine in terms of other doors that might be opened for him. As he liked to say, "The reward for a job well done is the opportunity to do more." (There was a minor side benefit to his notoriety that I once observed. He was pulled over by a policeman in the country outside of Pittsburgh. When the officer saw the name on my father's driver's license, he let him off with a warning instead of a ticket.)

I don't remember my father talking much with us kids about the work he was doing, though he certainly talked extensively with my mother (who helped him edit some of his papers). But one life-changing experience is seared into my memory. I recall sitting on a blanket with my father in the front yard during the summer of 1953. I was nine years old, and my father, for the first time, started talking to me in detail about the polio vaccine work he was doing. He talked about antibodies and the immune system, and showed me a variety of charts and graphs of the experimental results. I remember how well-organized and clear his ideas were, and how everything fell into place with the charts he showed me. I was struck by the feeling, in that moment, that someday I wanted to work with him.

My relationship with my father had its complexities. At times, when we talked together, he would be wrapped up in his own ideas and not fully open to my point of view. However, we had some extraordinary experiences when we finally did work together. I spent thirteen years at the Salk Institute, starting in 1972, and then worked with him on an HIV/AIDS vaccine project under the auspices of the Jonas Salk Foundation from 1991 until he died in 1995. I had some skills, perhaps similar to his, in making complex experimental results understandable in a graphic form. My father always valued what I did, and I felt the satisfaction of knowing that he fully appreciated my efforts. And when we worked together on various manuscripts, there was a unique way in which we were able to find a common ground that allowed our ideas to be expressed succinctly and effectively. I will always treasure those times with him.

There is a photo that beautifully illustrates this aspect of our relationship. It was taken in the small office I occupied when I was working with my father on the HIV/AIDS vaccine project. I don't recall what we were reviewing, but the delight on my father's face, and his total absorption in what he was reading, will always remain with me. Moments like those were precious—the very best part of the relationship we shared.

Peter L. Salk, MD, is president of the Jonas Salk Legacy Foundation and a professor of infectious diseases and microbiology at the University of Pittsburgh's Graduate School of Public Health. He lives in La Jolla, California, with his wife. They have one grown son.

My Father the Spy

Paul Dillon

by Eva Dillon

Paul Dillon was a Central Intelligence Agency case officer, born in Boston, Massachusetts, in 1927. He and his wife, Anne, had seven children, Maria, Clare, Eva, Julia, Leo, Paul, and Jacob. While working for the CIA at the height of the Cold War, Dillon was stationed in Germany, Mexico, Italy, and India. In 1975, after his cover was blown by a disgruntled former CIA case officer, the family returned to the United States. He died in 1980 at age fifty-three.

I WAS BORN IN WEST BERLIN IN 1957, the third of seven children. My father was posted there to deal with the threat of the Soviets surrounding this little enclave of the Allies. His cover was as US Army, but what he was actually doing was gathering information for the CIA from Soviets on the eastern side of the city. We lived in Berlin for about six years, and I have a vivid memory of my father taking me and my two older sisters to see the Berlin Wall. It had started going up a few weeks earlier, and he knew we would be hearing about it from other adults and at school, so he wanted to show it to us himself. I remember holding my father's hand and feeling frightened by the barbed wire and the scary-looking guards with guns and German shepherds. My father said, "Don't worry. Nothing will harm you. This is just a wall."

The qualities that made my dad a really good father were the same qualities that made him a good case officer. The most important thing between both a child and their parent and an asset and their handler is trust. My father engendered trust in everyone he knew because he saw the dignity in all people. Everyone, including us children, felt that from him. He was a devout Catholic and had attended a Jesuit high school and Jesuit-run Boston College. He was heavily influenced by the Jesuit vow of poverty, which can be interpreted as a vow to yourself that you are not better than anyone else. At work, when he was out of earshot, his colleagues affectionately referred to him as Father Paul.

He and my mother gave my siblings and me a lot of freedom growing up, and instilled in us a confidence that has stayed with us into adulthood. For instance, when we moved to India, all of us children were in our teens. My parents encouraged us to go see New Delhi on our own. We took rickshaws, exploring new and interesting neighborhoods. We would come home for dinner, and Dad would ask us, "Okay, what did you experience today?" He trusted us, and we did not want to betray his trust. We honored the faith and confidence he put in us by not getting into trouble.

He was also a lot of fun. With seven children, my mother needed a break sometimes. In Mexico, he took us to the Teotihuacán pyramids and to the bullfights. In Rome, we visited the catacombs, the Roman Forum, and the Pantheon. We were amazed that the rain fell right through the roof onto those beautiful marble floors. At the Bocca della Verità (the Mouth of Truth), a first-century Roman sculpture of a god's face, Dad explained that if you put your hand in the sculpture's mouth, it would bite it off if you told a lie.

My father was certainly under a lot of stress in those early Cold War years. While doing research for my book, *Spies in the Family*, I discovered interviews with my father's colleagues and documents that show the pressure he was under. For instance, in his first posting outside of Munich before I was born, he was responsible for training suitable refugees streaming into West Berlin from Eastern Europe in the face of Soviet occupation to parachute back into their own countries as spies for the Americans. But the operation was sabotaged from the start, and his recruits were being shot as soon as they landed. Though Dad didn't know it at the time, the infamous British spy Kim Philby—who had been working for the Russians for fifteen years while acting as the official intelligence liaison between the British and American intelligence services—was telegraphing the landing coordinates of my father's trained spies to Moscow. In a self-evaluation I later obtained, my father admitted that he was under considerable strain. As children, we had no idea.

Despite the pressure of my father's job, or perhaps because of it, my siblings and I were adept at entertaining him. For example, during the 1970s, the agency was weighted down with infighting, leaks, and suspicions driven by chief of Counterintelligence James Jesus Angleton, who believed that the CIA was seriously compromised by Soviet moles. My father was not one of Angleton's disciples, and he would come home drained from the pervasive sense of paranoia at the agency. At the time, my brothers had fallen in love with Monty Python. When Dad got home, they would re-create

Eva and Paul in West Berlin, 1957

scenes from *Life of Brian* wherein the various Judean fronts spent their energy fighting among themselves instead of against the common enemy, the Romans. My father would roar with laughter at these skits. In a way that my father understood, and my brothers did not, this was what was going on at the CIA.

In 1973, we moved to Delhi, India, so that my father could clandestinely handle one of the CIA's most valuable and highest-ranking assets, General Dmitri Polyakov. My father developed a close and strategically fruitful relationship with him. In the summer of 1975, when I was seventeen, a newspaper article in the *Times of India* identified my father as a CIA officer. This was how we kids found out he worked for the agency, and it was, naturally, a shock. (My mother knew what he did—in fact, he had once recruited her to deliver a package to a dead drop in a Berlin park. She was so nervous, she refused to do any more drops after that.) The book from which the *Times of India* article was drawn, *Inside the Company: CIA Diary*, was written by Philip Agee, a disgruntled former CIA officer who revealed the identities of 250 covert officers, including my father. It was, in a sense, the WikiLeaks exposé scandal of the 1970s.

But even after my dad's cover was publicly revealed, we still did not confront or ask him about it. We just knew he wouldn't want or be able to tell us what he was really doing at work every day. We respected and loved him too much to put him in an uncomfortable position by asking him.

It wasn't dangerous for my father in India after his cover was blown, since he had diplomatic immunity, but his career as a foreign operative was over. Soon he was posted back in the United States to work at Camp Peary, the CIA training complex in Virginia known as "The Farm." Shortly after our arrival in the States, Dad told us we needed to attend a meeting at the Camp Peary administrative base. When we arrived, we were all escorted into a conference room. There's a policy that the family of CIA officers living at Camp Peary are told that their parent is in the Agency, since the site's existence as a CIA training facility is an open secret. A camp administrator got straight to the point: "Does anyone here know what your father does for a living?" We were a little embarrassed because Dad had never said anything to us about his role directly, even after his cover was publicly blown in India, but we all admitted that we did. The moment was awkward. We were being forced to confront a lifetime of unspoken, brokered deception, of never revealing the truth on my father's part, of willful ignorance on ours. Our warm and loving father, who would deal honestly with us regarding any personal issue we wanted to discuss or problems we faced, was embarrassed, I believe, to have an official inform us that he worked for the CIA rather than do it himself. Yet the situation was telling: it was an example of my father's need to compartmentalize and yet stay true to the two institutions, the CIA and his family, to which he'd faithfully committed himself.

Another thing my father and mother shielded us from was the fact that he was dying. While we were in India, he had developed primary pulmonary hypertension, a narrowing and atrophying of the lungs' veins and capillaries. In the late '70s, the disease was fatal. (Today, it is treated with Viagra.) My siblings and I knew that Dad was sick but not how serious it was. Eventually, though, we realized that he was dying, even if we didn't face, or often discuss, how soon we would lose him.

Once again, we respected his cues and honored what we knew he wanted by not fully letting on that we were aware of his condition. If he didn't want to tell us he was dying, who were we to insist? After all, we loved our father, and we didn't want to blow his cover.

Eva Dillon spent twenty-five years in magazine publishing. In 2017, she released her first book, *Spies in the Family*, about her father and his relationship with General Dmitri Polyakov. She lives in Charleston, South Carolina, with her husband.

My Father the Stargazer Carl Sagan

by Nick Sagan

Born in Brooklyn, New York, in 1934, Carl Sagan was an astronomer, astrobiologist, astrophysicist, and author. Perhaps best known for writing and narrating Cosmos: A Personal Voyage, *the most-watched PBS series to date, Sagan was also a professor of astronomy at Cornell University, where he directed the Laboratory for Planetary Studies. He was married three times and had five children, Jeremy, Dorion, Nick, Alexandra, and Samuel. He died in 1996 at age sixty-two.*

A S MUCH AS I MISS MY FATHER, I can't help but take joy in knowing that I'm not alone in missing him. His work still awakens a sense of wonder in literally millions of people around the world, inspiring a lasting desire to learn about the cosmos. In this sense, he's more present in his absence than so many of us are in our presence. And though he was many things to many people, he was *my* dad, and I got to see the big thinker up close.

My father had a knack for pinball and knew just how hard to bump a machine without tilting it. When we'd go to arcades together, he'd win bonus games like mad. Video games, on the other hand, were never his thing. I remember the day I showed him Computer Baseball, a strategy game for the Apple II that came out in 1981. In the game, you could pit some of the greatest teams in MLB history against each other. We played Babe Ruth's 1927 Yankees against Jackie Robinson's 1955 Dodgers for about an hour. Then he turned to me and said, "Never show this to me again. I like it too much, and I don't want to lose time."

But he could and did—spend hours watching basketball. He was a huge fan. We'd watch NBA games whenever possible, wondering if this would be the year Patrick Ewing would lead the Knicks to the championship. (The answer was always no.) He'd point out the coaches and tell me what they were like as players back in the years before I was born. Dad never liked it when a visiting player went up to take a foul shot and the home team fans made noise and waved towels trying to distract him. He objected on principle—he didn't think it was sporting. There's something so decent about that.

I remember my mother getting increasingly upset one night in the summer of 1976. She wanted me to go to bed, but Dad and I were watching the NBA Finals. It was the Boston Celtics versus the Phoenix Suns. Dad had promised I could stay up until the end of

Game Five. Overtime. Then double overtime. Then triple overtime. Finally, the Celtics won, 128–126. Man, what a game.

My dad was a fantastic debater. He could, and did, take William F. Buckley Jr.'s politically conservative arguments apart when he appeared on Buckley's television show, *Firing Line*. When I was a kid, Dad and I frequently debated, too, but after my "Why you should buy me a cool dirt bike" argument failed to gain traction, I realized that my powers of persuasion didn't quite match up to Buckley's. But Dad always listened and gave me credit for making valid points. Often we'd find ourselves debating popular culture. For instance, he did not like the movie *Aliens*. I thought it was fun, scary, cathartic; he thought it was needlessly violent and wondered why extraterrestrials must be portrayed in such a negative light.

He had mixed feelings about *Star Wars*. I remember watching it with him, and when we reached the part where Han Solo brags that the *Millennium Falcon* made the Kessel Run in "less than twelve parsecs," he made an exasperated sound. I asked him what was wrong, and he explained that a parsec is a unit of distance, not time.

"Dad, it's just a movie," I said.

"Yes," he replied, "but they can afford to get the science right."

We argued about *The Simpsons* and *Beavis and Butt-Head*, which, as a kid, I loved. Both shows made a bad first impression on him. I persuaded him to give *The Simpsons* another chance, and he eventually saw what all the fuss was about and grew to genuinely enjoy it. I don't think I ever won him over on *Beavis and Butt-Head*, though. "They're not meant to be role models," I protested. "It's a subversive critique." Nope, not his cup of tea. But he was a big fan of David Lean epics like *Doctor Zhivago* and, especially, *Lawrence of Arabia*. He loved that transition where Peter O'Toole blows out the match and the film cuts quite suddenly to the Nafud desert.

One of the things about my father that makes me smile even today is remembering the interesting noises he made. His laugh was explosive and uninhibited—the kind of laugh that made you feel good for making him laugh. His sneezes were booming. And sometimes he'd talk to animals in their native tongue. When we'd see

Carl and Nick (four years old) in Ithaca, New York, 1974

dolphins at the aquarium, he'd greet them in a reasonable approximation of dolphin speak. (They'd often answer him. I have no idea what they said.) But my favorite sound of his was the one he'd make upon discovering something intriguing and new, some idea or possibility that impressed him or opened up a fresh way of looking at things. It was a kind of "aaah." One of my proudest moments was when we were watching "Attached," the first episode of *Star Trek: Deep Space Nine* I had written. Within minutes of the opening credits, my dad made that "aaah" sound. Turning to me with a beaming smile, he said, "That's really good, Nick." And this continued for the entire show. The completeness of how much he loved what I'd done, that genuine sense of enjoyment, stays with me. It gave me a sense of respect and approval I treasure like nothing else.

Nick Sagan is a novelist and screenwriter. He lives in Ithaca, New York, with his wife and daughter.

My
Father
the
Strongman
Jack
LaLanne

by Jon LaLanne

Born François Henri LaLanne in San Francisco, California, in 1914, Jack LaLanne is considered the father of fitness in the United States. He opened the first health and fitness club in the country in Oakland in 1936. For thirty-four years starting in 1951, he preached the gospel of healthy eating and regular exercise on The Jack LaLanne Show. *He was renowned for his feats of strength, such as swimming from Alcatraz Island to Fisherman's Wharf in San Francisco handcuffed, shackled, and towing a half-ton boat. (He was sixty years old.) LaLanne had four children, Yvonne, Janet, Daniel, and Jon. He died in 2011, at age ninety-six.*

Jack and Jon (seven years old) on the set of *The Jack LaLanne Show*, 1968

I GREW UP WITH A SILVER SPOON and my father's iron fist in the Hollywood Hills. When I was a kid, in the 1960s, Dad was at the height of his fame, so he wasn't around all that much. But of course, I'd see him every day on *The Jack LaLanne Show*. And he ran a very tight ship, especially when it came to health, regardless of whether he was home. He was a fanatic. For breakfast, I was given a brown shake made of desiccated liver tablets, cod oil, and vitamins instead of bacon and eggs. At school, all the kids would have Ding Dongs and Twinkies in their lunch boxes. I'd have an apple. I'd desperately try to trade, but with little luck. On my eleventh birthday, my dad got me a whole wheat birthday cake. You couldn't cut it with a chain saw! His fanaticism wasn't directed at only us kids, either. My parents would host dinner parties, and he'd always be lecturing their guests: that they should eat healthier, work out more, and stay active. Lecturing. Lecturing. Lecturing.

Naturally, I spent most of my childhood trying to find a way to eat junk food. I'd raid the cabinets of our neighbors, the Boyers, who lived at the end of the cul-de-sac and kept boxes of Count Chocula and Cap'n Crunch in their house. I even wrangled an invite to Camp Israel, where I was probably the only person there for the food and was certainly the only goy. But mostly I relied on our housekeeper, Hattie. With Dad gone and Mom busy, I spent a lot of time alone with her. As strict as my father was, Hattie tried to soften the edges and make sure my childhood wasn't all juice and lectures. She was a real pioneer when it came to healthy cooking, too. She started making the soul food she grew up with in a way that would meet Dad's strict guidelines. She'd make potato chips in safflower oil and with sea salt, fried chicken with a whole wheat batter, and custard sweetened with honey. But she didn't do everything by the book. She kept a secret cabinet for my siblings and me filled with dehydrated space food and Snack Pack pudding. And sometimes she'd sneak me down to C.C. Brown's on Hollywood Boulevard, where we'd get hot fudge sundaes—scoops of vanilla ice cream in a silver bowl with hot fudge poured on top and a cloud of whipped cream. But the holy grail, for really special occasions, was McDonald's french fries.

Though he was strict, Dad was also a comedian. When he was at home, he was cracking jokes 24/7. He wasn't an angry guy, and he got on well with everybody (as long as you didn't mind being lectured about health and fitness). In his mind, the most important thing he could do was deliver the message to the American people that fitness and diet matter, and that mission cut across all sorts of cultural lines. In the 1960s and '70s, a lot of hippies used to come hang out at our house, attracted to Dad's gospel of healthy eating. (Meanwhile, I had to sneak over to the Boyers' to smoke pot, terrified of Dad ever finding out.) I'm not sure what the flower children made of my dad, who always wore his trademark jumpsuit and his hair close-cropped, or what he made of them, in their bell-bottoms and tie-dye, but they at least saw eye to eye on the virtues of nonprocessed food.

As for me, I had to leave home and go out on my own—and pass some years with terrible digestive health—to finally discover that Dad was pretty much right. I'll never forget those hot fudge sundaes and forbidden french fries, but these days I have a healthy shake every morning and exercise daily. Just like he would have wanted.

_____

Jon LaLanne is a surfboard builder, entrepreneur, artist, and musician. He lives on the Big Island of Hawaii with his wife, two dogs, and two cats.

My Father the Superman

Christopher Reeve

by Matthew Reeve

Born in New York City in 1952, Christopher Reeve was an actor best known for his starring role in the 1978 film Superman *and its sequels; his career spanned Broadway and television as well. In 1995, he was injured in a horse-riding accident that left him paralyzed from the neck down. He continued to work, directing the movie* In the Gloaming *and starring in a remake of* Rear Window *for which he won a SAG Award; writing a bestselling memoir,* Still Me; *and raising money for spinal cord injury research, establishing the Christopher and Dana Reeve Foundation. Reeve had three children, Matthew, Alexandra, and Will. He died in 2004 at age fifty-two.*

Christopher and Matthew (four years old) with their dog, Bonjour, in London, 1983

I WAS BORN just a year after my father's first Superman film came out, when he went from being a relatively unknown actor to one of the biggest movie stars in the world almost overnight. So much of my early life was bound up in the fame and attention that came from that franchise. And although the rest of the world thought of him as that character, to me, he was just Dad. And what I remember most was what he did offscreen.

Prior to his accident, my father was an incredibly athletic man, a highly skilled sailor, an accomplished pianist, and an avid pilot. By the time he was twenty-three, he had flown across the United States in a little Cessna 172, landing in fields and sleeping under the wings before setting off again. Later, he crossed the Atlantic twice.

I was fifteen when my father was paralyzed. My sister, Alexandra, was eleven. My brother, Will, was almost three. (In fact, we celebrated his third birthday in the ICU of the University of Virginia Medical Center, where my dad had been airlifted immediately after the accident.) So while my brother doesn't remember my father being able-bodied, my sister and I do. Some of my earliest, fondest memories with him involve airplanes. We used to drive up to Teterboro, New Jersey, where he kept a small twin-engine turbo-prop. And from there we would fly out to Martha's Vineyard or up to Vermont or Massachusetts, where we had family.

I remember once, when we were in London (where my sister and I mostly grew up—all the Superman films were shot at Pinewood Studios), sitting in the passenger seat of his bright purple Triumph TR6 convertible, with black leather seats, a walnut-paneled dash, and a chrome gear stick. The top was down, and my dad—all six feet four inches of him, in his prime and at the height of his career—was like an eyeball magnet. Everyone looked as we drove by. We were headed to an airfield on the edge of town where we'd hop in an old World War II biplane with an open cockpit and cruise around the skies. In retrospect, I mean, how cool is that? But to six-year-old me, it was just another weekend with my dad.

When we were in his plane, more often than not I'd sit next to him in the copilot seat. A plane is not like a car: Sitting in the copilot's seat, you have the controls right there in front of you, within reach, and the throttle and the gauges, too. You can really make things go wrong if you don't do exactly as instructed. But Dad started giving me responsibility from an early age. He'd have me lower the flaps for landing or raise the landing gear after takeoff. There was so much to learn. When we were in the air, there wasn't a lot of chitchat, because you're always on the Air Traffic Control radio. But sitting there, side by side, thousands of feet off the ground, was the best father-son bonding a boy could ever ask for.

When I was six years old, my mother, Gae, and my father split up and Dad moved to New York to live full-time. He soon met Dana, an amazing woman who would become very dear to me. They eventually married, and when I was twelve, they had Will and moved to Westchester County in New York. My sister and I were still going to school in England, but we visited every break.

Around that time, my dad got back into horse riding, which he had learned years earlier for his role as Count Vronsky in *Anna Karenina*. Westchester was horse country, and my dad, who was always active, became more involved in the sport. Over Memorial Day weekend in 1995, he went down to Culpeper, Virginia, for a three-day competition. During the second day's cross-country event, his horse stopped suddenly in front of an obstacle and my dad's momentum carried him forward, over the horse's head and onto the ground. For some reason, he couldn't break his fall with his hands (perhaps they were entangled in the reins—at least that's the story I've heard). He landed on his head, and the impact shattered his first and second cervical vertebrae. Thankfully, there was an off-duty EMT at the event who performed an emergency tracheotomy so my dad could breathe. Then he was airlifted to Charlottesville.

I was staying in London alone at the time, while my mother and sister were in Hampshire. Dana called the house super early on

Sunday morning and asked if my mom was there. I said she wasn't. Dana, trying not to alarm me, told me that my dad had had a little accident and hurt his neck and that she was going to call my mom. Dana hung up, and a few minutes later my mom called me and told me to pack a bag for the airport. By the time we left on Monday, news of my dad's accident had gone public. I remember actually first learning of the gravity of the situation from the front pages of the newspapers at the airport. The press reported that my father's condition was very touch and go and his survival was uncertain. At the same time, I was a savvy schoolboy—or so I thought—who knew that papers were just trying to sell copies, so I was hoping, somehow, that the stories were all sensationalized. That his injuries weren't as serious as they said.

But of course they were. For the first four to five weeks after the accident, we didn't know if my dad was going to live through the night. Although he stabilized, and eventually was able to move to a rehabilitation facility in New Jersey, then, six months later, finally return home, I'd estimate that during that period, he flatlined three or four times. Meanwhile, letters would arrive at the hospital by the boxful from all across the world. One I remember, from England, was addressed simply, "Superman, USA." We would open these letters and hold them up to his face so he could read them. Often they were notes of sympathy and support. Some people wrote of fellow loved ones who had been paralyzed or injured, and offered advice and guidance. Others would say anything they could think of to try to relate to him. They sent introductions to shamans and doctors, little trinkets and charms, and pictures of themselves. The love my father received from the public was a little bit overwhelming, but it gave him strength and motivation to keep going.

After Dad's accident, obviously, there was no more flying, no more sailing, no more buzzing through London in a Triumph with the top down. By necessity, our father-son bonding became much more verbal. We would sit and talk, something we never did before. We were still navigating journeys together, just this time on the ground.

Even before he returned home, Dad became involved in helping others with spinal cord injuries. He was so driven to find a cure, he became obsessed. He knew he could use his celebrity to raise awareness—and donations—and become a voice for a whole community of people who didn't really have one. Every night, he was either on the phone with researchers, corresponding with other people with spinal cord injuries and giving them advice on how to keep going, talking with policymakers, or trying to navigate the tangled bureaucratic web of insurance companies. He was data driven, and just as he used to pore over his thick book of flight maps, planning approaches to various airports, he now assiduously read up on the latest scientific developments related to his injury. And he was eager to tell everyone what he learned. In fact, he was so passionate about it that Dana ultimately banned all research conversation from the dinner table.

As his son, I could see both how different he was after the accident, how his physical body and all that he could do narrowed dramatically in scope, and also that his spirit—curious, indomitable, charismatic, kind—was never broken. When he was first injured, no one was sure what lay ahead—least of all him. I was privileged to bear witness to an amazing evolution as he found and harnessed an incredible inner strength and resolve to carry on and do what he did. A couple of years before he died, I made a documentary with my father about his journey after the accident. His final lines in that film resonate with me. He says, "Everyone always tells me I'm such an inspiration. I don't know about that. I try to emphasize that the ability to endure, the ability to love, is something we all have inside us, and you don't have to be a Superman to do it."

Matthew Reeve is a filmmaker, producer, and director. Along with his sister and brother, he serves on the board of the Christopher and Dana Reeve Foundation. He lives in Stockholm, Sweden, with his partner and their two children.

My Father the Visionary Eero Saarinen

by Eric Saarinen

Eero Saarinen, born in Kirkkonummi, Finland, in 1910, was an influential architect and designer. A pioneer in the mid-century modern aesthetic, Saarinen is perhaps best known for his designs of the Gateway Arch in Saint Louis, the TWA Flight Center in New York City, and the Dulles International Airport in Washington, DC. Working with the furniture company Knoll, he designed some of the most iconic pieces of the twentieth century, including the Tulip Womb Chair. Saarinen, who died at age fifty-one in 1961, had three children, Eric, Susan, and Eames.

Eric (age three) with Eero, 1945

M Y FATHER WAS ALWAYS COMPETING with his father, Eliel, a world-famous Finnish architect whom I called Farfar. Eliel had moved the family to the United States in 1923 to design, build, and teach at the Cranbrook Academy of Art in Bloomfield Hills, Michigan. He and my grandmother Loja, whom I called Mormor, had two children, my aunt Pipsan, who became a textile and furniture designer, and my father, who became an architect. By the time I was born, in 1942, my father was working with Farfar at his firm, Saarinen, Swansen and Associates, but was making a name for himself, too, in particular with his collaborations with his friend Charles Eames.

I was five years old when my father won the competition to design the Gateway Arch in Saint Louis. He and his father had entered the competition separately. They had built a divider that ran the length of their shared office at Cranbrook. My father worked on one side, assisted by Charles, and my grandfather worked on the other. My dad's design was a catenary arch, and I remember that at this time, our basement had a bunch of chains hanging from the ceiling that my dad used to figure out the shape. When he won, the telegram was sent to his father, congratulating him on his design. Farfar and the office celebrated for three days straight. On the third day, the phone rang at my grandparents' house. It was George Howe, the head of the jury. "I'm sorry," he told Farfar. "My secretary got confused. That telegram was meant for your son, the other E. Saarinen." That was a big moment in my father and grandfather's relationship.

Farfar was a huge part of my dad's life and a huge part of my life, too. In fact, my earliest memories are of him coming up to me and poking his finger into my stomach. He made a *pfffft* noise like a balloon and I would laugh and laugh. He was a generous teacher and gifted at inspiring others. He had a great sense of humor and was totally devoted to his family. He was everything my father wasn't.

Mormor was a part-German, part-Swedish, part-Finnish sculptor. She was very organized, very Teutonic. She designed her own clothes and ran Cranbrook's weaving department. But she was also extremely supportive of her husband. My dad was always looking for a wife like Mormor. When he met my mom, Lilian, he thought she was perfect. She was a beautiful woman, funny and full of intuition. She was a member of the first US Women's Olympic Alpine Ski Team in 1936, but her true passion was art. She used to go to the Detroit Zoo to paint, sculpt, and draw the animals. As my father would eventually find out, however, she also suffered from chemical imbalances and depression. And then, when I was about three, she contracted tuberculosis and went to live at a sanatorium. We didn't see her for three years. My father was so busy at the time, we hardly ever saw him, either. Instead we lived with friends of my maternal grandparents. We didn't spend time with either our mother or our father during that period except once, when my father took us to the sanatorium to wave hello at our mother, fifty yards away on the screened-in porch.

When my mother came back, she was taking Seconal to sleep and drinking at the same time. That was a bad combination. My mother hired a nanny to help cook and do laundry and take care of us while my father was at work, but he said that she could barely manage us even then. Still worse, in his eyes, was that she was more interested in her own art than in his. She loved my dad, but she wasn't Mormor.

When I was eleven, Aline Bernstein, a writer for the *New York Times*, took the train to Detroit to write a profile of my father. She was a real knockout. She and my father had an immediate, deep connection. I later found out that they slept together that very night. Soon after they met, I walked into our home to see my mother packing boxes. She was in tears.

"What's going on?" I asked.

"Your father and I are divorcing," she replied, "and he is kicking us out of the house."

I think Aline wanted my mother as far away as possible. My father, meanwhile, made my mom file for divorce—even though she didn't want to—because he thought it would look bad if he was the one who filed. I hated my father for a long time because of that.

Though my sister and I lived with my mother, she drank a lot, and eventually my father and Aline insisted I attend a boarding school. Once, when I was a teenager, my dad came to the school. He asked me what I wanted to do, what my interests were, and I told him I was in the chess club. So we played chess, and he systematically beat me over and over again. Then he left.

Soon I went away for college. But during the summer, I worked at Dad's architecture firm back in Michigan. I quickly found that I wasn't passionate about architecture. However, by the end of the summer, I had saved up enough money to buy a car, and I decided to leave. My plan was to drive to Cape Cod, where my mom and sister were spending the summer. I asked my father for permission. He said absolutely not. Aline intervened. "He's not going to crash," she said, "and if he gets into trouble, he'll figure out how to deal with the situation."

I got to Cape Cod with only a few misadventures. But shortly after I arrived, Aline called. "Get on a plane and come out to Bloomfield Hills," she told me. I did. When I arrived at the house, my dad was reading a book about Michelangelo and mumbling.

"Let's go to the Bloomfield Hills Hunt Club," suggested Aline. We had never been there in our lives, but I said okay. When we got to the club, I stretched out on a cot by the pool. Then Aline put an eye mask over my eyes and a blanket over my body. "Just wait here," she said. "Your father will be right over."

I remained there, wondering what was going to happen. Eventually I heard his footsteps on the pool deck and a little bit of scuffling and some whimpering. Then I heard my father mumbling, "I can't," and shuffling off. A few minutes later, Aline came back over, removed the eye mask, and told me to go back to Cape Cod. I was very confused but didn't question what had happened. It was just another instance of my father being inscrutable.

A few weeks later, I was back in Cape Cod when Aline called again to tell me my father had a brain tumor and was going into surgery.

There was a one-in-ten-thousand chance he would survive. That's what he couldn't do. He couldn't tell me he was dying. Shortly after, she called back and said he was dead. I started laughing, laughing at the irony that I—who hated him—now had to walk down the path to the ocean and tell my mother, the person who really loved him, that he had died. I was quiet for a full year after that. I was wounded and felt a lot of shame. I had very low self-esteem. My dad had died, and I couldn't do anything to make him proud or change the fact that he was gone. Our relationship, which had always been strained, would forever be left unresolved. For a long time, I was lost, but eventually I found my way to my own art.

I became a filmmaker and cinematographer. I shot film for *Gimme Shelter* and *Jimi Plays Berkeley*. I worked with Roger Corman on *Death Race 2000* and with Wes Craven on *The Hills Have Eyes*. This work, I felt, gave me some sort of validation. Each film proved *I was there*. Then, fifty years after my father died, I decided to make a documentary about him. It was called *Eero Saarinen: The Architect Who Saw the Future*. As I began researching my father, I found a trove of love letters between him and Aline that she had donated to the Smithsonian. Reading those letters was like taking uppers and downers at the same time. My father and Aline were drawn to each other—to hell with my mother. But Aline was good for him; she got him on the cover of *Time* magazine. Being with her was the only practical way for him personally and professionally to find happiness, and yet he sacrificed us for it.

For the first time, making the film, I really saw my father's brilliance. I used all my skills as a filmmaker to document his work. I even shot in 6K, a resolution so high you can't yet project it. But I wasn't just shooting for now. I was shooting for the future. My dad always said what he wanted was to be part of the history of architecture, and I'm happy that's something I helped preserve.

Eric Saarinen is a director and cinematographer who lives in Harbor City, California. He is working on a film about his grandfather Eliel.

My Father the Voice

Jim Cummings

by Raleigh West

James Jonah Cummings, born in Youngstown, Ohio, in 1952, is one of America's greatest voice actors. Over the last forty years, he has given voice to Winnie the Pooh, Taz the Tasmanian Devil, and hundreds of other iconic characters. He most recently supplied the voice of Winnie the Pooh in the live-action Disney film Christopher Robin. *He is the father of four daughters, Livia, Raleigh, Gracie, and Lulu.*

Raleigh (seven months old) and Jim, 1987

L IKE EVERY OTHER KID, I grew up watching cartoons. But unlike most other kids, I often heard my father's voice coming from the television. My dad seemed to be on just about every program, voicing such characters as Darkwing Duck and Dr. Robotnik in *Sonic the Hedgehog*, Mickey's nemesis Pete on *Goof Troop*, Cat from *CatDog*, and Winnie the Pooh, one of the most beloved characters in all of children's literature. His voices were different for each character, obviously, but I always knew when I heard Dad.

We—my sister, Livia; my dad; my mom; and I—lived in a ranch-style house in the Santa Rosa Valley in Camarillo, California. It's horse country, and there were trails all over the neighborhood and a creek at the end of our cul-de-sac. Livia and I grew up outside, making tree houses and getting into trouble. When the sun went down, my dad would whistle for us to come in for dinner. It was like an arrow shot across the land. He had a unique whistle for each of us—the one for me was a sort of four-note phrase using my first and middle name: Ra-leigh-JACK-son; the one for my sister was a triplet: Li-vi-a!—and as soon as we heard it, we'd race back home. Funny for the daughter of a voice actor, but my dad's whistle is what really sticks in my mind.

As one of the most in-demand voice actors of the '80s, Dad worked constantly when I was a kid. He frequently left for the studio before we got up and returned late at night. I always loved when his recording schedule allowed him to take me to school. And he had great kid advice: "Have too much fun." "Instincts are the best stinks." "Ask the questions and question the answers." The last piece of advice I took so much to heart that I was told by more than one teacher that I asked too many questions. Dad categorically denied that this was possible.

He was an excellent storyteller. He once told us about when he was working on a tugboat in New Orleans and something went wrong when the boat was going through the locks. Locks are essentially water elevators used to navigate boats down the Mississippi River. The water was emptying to take the boat down a level. Dad and the other deckhands needed to untie the boat from the docks so it could go down with the water level, but a rope on one side was stuck. The water was lowering, but that side of the boat wasn't. The boat started tipping on its side and threatening to capsize. According to Dad, he raced to the galley, grabbed a cleaver, ran back to the line, and cut it free just before certain disaster. I was enthralled by this story as a kid and was convinced that it was completely true. My father was a hero for sure.

Our home was always filled with stories, music, and art. My mother was a gifted stained-glass artist before becoming a full-time mom, and she was constantly working on some project to decorate the house. Re-covering the furniture, framing old family photos, or arranging our artwork. Every time she'd decide to change the wall color, Dad would take the opportunity to paint on the walls with us before she covered them with a new shade. My sister and I loved to doodle on the walls while Dad created big murals of leafy greenery. Any opportunity to be creative and fun and feel a little like a trouble-maker, he jumped at.

Right after I turned thirteen, my parents got divorced. It was messy. My sister and I would go for months without contact with our dad. Normally when you don't speak to someone, you don't hear their voice at all, but that wasn't the case for us. I'd be over at a friend's house, and my dad would be selling us Cheez-Its during the commercial break. We'd be driving in the car, and we'd hear Dad telling us to buy a Lexus. Someone could be watching TV two rooms away, and I'd all of a sudden turn and say, "That's my dad." I can tell if it's him just by how he clears his throat. It's like a homing beacon. I'm not conscious of it, but my ear turns my head and I can't help but say, "That's my dad." I interrupt whoever is talking. No "Excuse me," just a quick "That's my dad." It's a compulsion. I still do it. It's a bit of a heart-break when the voice of someone you're angry at comes into your space so often, but such was life for my sister and me as teenagers.

Things eventually settled down, and we began to reconnect with him. We all went to Disneyland together a few years ago when he was working at D23, the Disney Convention. I was waiting for him to go to lunch in the lobby of the Grand Californian. It's an enormous Arts-and-Crafts-style hotel with fifty-foot-high ceilings, kids and families everywhere, cartoons playing on an old-timey TV. I was in a chair staring at my phone in the middle of all this when I found myself suddenly standing and looking three stories up toward the elevators and the third-story rooms. My dad was standing there, grinning from ear to ear in shock and amazement. He had done my whistle, the one that he once used to call me home from playing outside as a kid. I hadn't even realized it till I saw his face! It was like I was a sleeper agent programmed as a child to come to this whistle. I stood up and looked before my brain even registered it. Neither of us could believe that it had worked, so many years later and across a crowded hotel lobby. I looked up at him, he looked down at me, and we shared a laugh, bridging the distance and years between us.

Raleigh West is a professional organizer and storyteller who lives in Los Angeles, California.

My Father the Vulcan

Leonard Nimoy

by Adam Nimoy

Leonard Nimoy was born in Boston, Massachusetts, in 1931. As an actor, he is best known for his portrayal of Mr. Spock, the half-Vulcan, half-human, hyperlogical first officer aboard the starship Enterprise *on Star Trek. He was also a poet, director, photographer, and philanthropist. In 1954, he married Sandra Zober, with whom he had two children, Adam and Julie. The couple divorced in 1987, and in 1989, he married actress Susan Bay, who played Admiral Rollman in* Star Trek: Deep Space Nine. *He died in 2015 at age eighty-three.*

I ARRIVED LATE TO THE LECTURE. It was the fall of my senior year at UC Berkeley, and my father was making a personal appearance at Wheeler Hall in front of three hundred mesmerized students. During the 1970s, Dad made a number of paid college appearances where he would talk about *Star Trek*, his work in the theater, his recording career, and his photography. Having lived through all of this, I didn't need to be at the lecture from the start, so I quietly slid into a seat in the back of the auditorium halfway through and waited for him to finish. We hadn't seen each other since I had been home the previous summer, and in the three years I had been away at school, Dad had never come to visit. His appearance at Cal gave us the opportunity to have dinner together. I was looking forward to it, despite knowing in my gut that it was the fans, not me, that had finally brought him to Berkeley.

When the talk was over and he was done signing autographs, I waved to Dad. He walked up the aisle toward me. We had barely finished hugging when he hit me with a sucker punch.

"I can't go to dinner after all," he said. "I have a commitment in the morning. There's a car waiting for me, and I'm already late for my plane."

That was it. He walked out the door.

Devastated but not surprised, I pushed down my feelings like I had done so many times before. But his behavior made perfectly clear something I had struggled with all of my life: Dad's career came first.

Later, when I told my sister, Julie, what had happened, she said that Dad was being passive-aggressive because he was in competition with me. "What are you talking about?" I asked, incredulously. How could my father possibly see me as a threat?

Star Trek was exploding in TV syndication, and college campuses like mine were epicenters of *Star Trek* mania. Berkeley even boasted the Federation Trading Post, a store where you could buy all things

Trek, including a photo of me standing with Dad on the bridge of the *Enterprise* sporting a Spock haircut and a pair of his pointed ears. Every weekday at 5:00 p.m., my fellow students would cram into dormitory TV rooms all over campus to watch reruns of the show. With the popularity of Spock soaring, Dad was a bona fide star, a Vulcan sex symbol. I remember seeing women attempt to kiss him when we were out in public—sometimes successfully. I didn't understand how my father could possibly see us as competitors.

"Dad barely made it through high school," Julie reminded me.

"And?" I asked.

"And being Russian immigrants, Nana and Papa always dreamed he would go to college. Now that you're at Cal, he's flat-out jealous." At that moment, I began to understand my father a little better.

Dad had to grow up fast during the Depression. The son of a barber, he supplemented the family income by selling newspapers in the Boston Common at age ten. In 1949, when he was eighteen, he traveled alone cross-country to find fame and fortune in Los Angeles. Success didn't come easy. He drove a cab, serviced gumball machines, and scooped ice cream to make ends meet, all the while honing his craft in dozens of bit parts in film and on TV. Everything changed in the fall of 1966 when the TV-watching public decided that Mr. Spock was one of the coolest characters ever to hit the airwaves. From then on, his life was all about the work and the publicity and the personal appearances and all those fans.

When Dad did spend time with me, it was often awkward. Unlike him, as a kid, I didn't contribute to the family income. Instead, I was listening to the Beatles, reading Spider-Man comics, and watching TV. None of that seemed to interest him. Our real clashes began in the mid-'70s when I was working hard in school while living on a steady diet of cannabis and the Grateful Dead. Dad couldn't tolerate it. Sure, there were some wonderful moments, like the time he took me to the press conference to announce *Star Trek: The Motion Picture* or the time he went bonkers when I told him that I had managed to pass the California bar exam on my first try. But he was drinking and

Adam (age nine) and Leonard on the set of *Star Trek*, 1966

I was using, and this fueled episodes of conflict in which we simply lacked any tools to break the cycle.

For most of my adult life, this pattern of conflict followed by total estrangement marked my relationship with my father. But the turning point came in 2006 after he wrote a six-page letter outlining all of my shortcomings with an emphasis on how, through the years, I had taken advantage of his largesse. By that time, I had been sober for two years (my dad had been sober for six), and I thought I was practicing the principle of "contrary action"—a core tenet of twelve-step programs in which one does the opposite of their habitual impulse—by refusing to respond to a letter that cut me straight to the bone.

But when I told the story of the letter, and my pride at ignoring it, my sponsor, who knew me well, said, "Not so fast." He agreed that what my father had done was not so great for his own recovery. He knew I could find plenty of people who would agree that what he had done was wrong. But he also believed that the letter presented me with a choice: I could be right or I could be happy. He told me that I had let the conflict with my father define much of my life, and that if I wanted to achieve the recovery objective of being "happy, joyous, and free," I should take that letter and make an amends to him for everything in it. I was shocked.

When I finally caught my breath, I balked at this—fought it, even—reminding my sponsor that during the course of my father's sobriety, he had never made an amends to me. The amends wasn't for him, he assured me. It was for me and my recovery.

I could be right or I could be happy. So I took that letter and met with my father at his big house in Bel Air and made the amends to him, and it sucked. Without qualification or hesitation, I read through the entire six pages of grievances and apologized to him for all the mistakes I had made and all the things I had said and done that were hurtful to him. He just sat there listening. By the time I left his house, I was crushed.

But lo and behold, things started to change. What followed was an almost immediate period of rapprochement in which Dad and I began building a bridge to each other. We started talking regularly and even attended AA meetings together. When my second wife, Martha, was diagnosed with terminal cancer, my father was there for me every step of the way. I could always count on him during moments of crisis when I just needed someone to talk to. This was his amends to me. In recovery, it's referred to as a living amends. From that point on, until the day my father died, we focused on building a loving relationship and never again looked back at the wreckage of our past.

Adam Nimoy is a director and author. He has directed over forty-five hours of network television, and his films include *Leonard Nimoy's Boston* and *For the Love of Spock*. He is the author of *My Incredibly Wonderful, Miserable Life: An Anti-Memoir*. He has three children and two stepchildren and lives in Los Angeles, California, with his wife.

Acknowledgments

THIS COLLECTION would not have been possible without the generous contributions of the sons and daughters who graciously shared their stories. They weren't always easy to tell and, even if they were joyous, still took a tremendous amount of effort to form. So I want to thank the forty men and women in these pages for their courage, openness, generosity and heart. I'd also like to thank the teams at Fatherly—including Mike Rothman, Andrew Burmon, Lizzy Francis, Tyghe Trimble, Amy Karafin, Patrick Coleman, and Anne Meadow—and at Artisan, including Lia Ronnen, Elise Ramsbottom, Sibylle Kazeroid, Jane Treuhaft, Toni Tajima, Nancy Murray, and the Brooklyn Cyclones' greatest fan, Bridget Monroe Itkin.

About the Authors

Joshua David Stein is the editor at large at Fatherly. He is also a coauthor of *Notes from a Young Black Chef, Il Buco Essentials,* and *Food & Beer* and the author of five children's books, including *Can I Eat That?* and *What's Cooking?* The father of two sons, he lives in Brooklyn, New York.

Fatherly is the leading digital media brand for dads. Its mission is to empower men to raise great kids and enjoy more fulfilling adult lives.

Library of Congress Cataloging-in-Publication Data
Names: Stein, Joshua David, author.
Title: To me, he was just dad / Joshua David Stein.
Description: New York City : Artisan, a division of Workman Publishing Co., Inc., 2020.
Identifiers: LCCN 2019048609 | ISBN 9781579659349 (hardcover)
Subjects: LCSH: Fathers and sons—Anecdotes.
Classification: LCC HQ755.85 S7395 2020 | DDC 306.874/2—dc23
LC record available at https://lccn.loc.gov/2019048609

Design by Toni Tajima
Cover design by Michelle Ishay-Cohen
Cover and interior lettering by Kirby Salvador

Artisan books are available at special discounts when purchased in bulk for premiums and sales promotions as well as for fund-raising or educational use. Special editions or book excerpts also can be created to specification. For details, contact the Special Sales Director at the address below, or send an e-mail to specialmarkets@workman.com.

For speaking engagements, contact speakersbureau@workman.com.

Published by Artisan
A division of Workman Publishing Co., Inc.
225 Varick Street
New York, NY 10014-4381
artisanbooks.com

Artisan is a registered trademark of Workman Publishing Co., Inc.

Published simultaneously in Canada by Thomas Allen & Son, Limited

Printed in China

First printing, March 2020

1 3 5 7 9 10 8 6 4 2